A HISTORY OF OXFORDSHIRE

*Oxfordshire County
Council arms*

Wroxton, north Oxfordshire, one of many pretty villages in the county.

THE DARWEN COUNTY HISTORY SERIES

A History of Oxfordshire

MARY JESSUP

Cartography by ROY MOLE
Drawings by ALISON CRAWFORD

PHILLIMORE

First published 1975
by
PHILLIMORE & CO. LTD.
London and Chichester

Head Office: Shopwyke Hall,
Chichester, Sussex, England

ISBN 0 85033 206 0

Printed in Great Britain by
UNWIN BROTHERS LIMITED
at The Gresham Press, Old Woking, Surrey

Contents

*Whispering Knights
dolmen, Great
Rollright*

Maps

The Tolsey, Burford

List of Plates

Acknowledgements

All the coloured illustrations are published by courtesy of Mr. J. W. Thomas, Thomas-Photos, Oxford. The courtesy of the following is gratefully acknowledged for permission to publish illustrations: the Ashmolean Museum (nos. 1, 3, 5, 11, 34, 43, 44), all from the collection of Major George Allen; the Bodleian Library (nos. 4, 13-16, 18-21, 26, 27, 29-33, 35, 36, 41); The Royal Agricultural Society of England (no. 39); Oxford County Libraries (nos. 2, 12, 37, 38, 45), all from the collection of Henry Taunt. I am grateful to George Smith for nos. 8, 9, 10, and 28 which are reproductions of engravings in J. Skelton, *The Antiquities of Oxfordshire*, and nos. 7, 23, 24, 25, and 42, from J. Ingram, *Memorials of Oxford*. Nos. 6 and 46 are from photographs by Mr. J. Griffiths; no. 40 is from *Punch*, 9, Sept. 1865.

The maps numbered XIII are based on a map in the possession of Oriel College and upon the Ordnance Survey Map with the sanction of the Controller of H. M. Stationery Office. Crown Copyright reserved.

Preface

This book is concerned with the county of Oxford as it was before the reorganisation of local government and the consequent boundary changes brought into effect on 1 April 1974.

Oxfordshire was not intended to form a natural unit when the boundary was first laid out late in the 9th or early in the 10th century A.D. and for this reason alone there is nothing homogeneous about the county even after a thousand years or more of its existence. Oxfordshire was, until recently, completely overshadowed by its county town. With the growth of Banbury and the tendency of people in and around Henley-on-Thames to look to London and Reading for their livelihood, dependence on Oxford has consequently decreased. The city of Oxford was, in turn, dominated for centuries by an extremely powerful and influential University. So great was this domination that the presence in Oxford of a quite separate group of people—the townsfolk—was almost lost to view. This situation has been rectified to a large extent by local government reform in the 19th century, and in the last 50 years or so, by rapid industrial development. In this book an attempt has been made to keep these three parts of Oxfordshire—Town, Gown, and County—more equal in importance.

To write a purely chronological history of Oxfordshire which is not a disjointed mixture of facts and subjects is probably impossible. That is why this History has been divided up into topics, which it is hoped, while not being an ideal arrangement, at least gives some clarity to what is a highly complicated and complex story.

It is, of course, an anachronism to write of 'Oxfordshire' as a territorial unit in Prehistoric, Roman, and early Anglo-Saxon times. Its use in the first few chapters is more convenient for author and reader alike than any alternative term.

I am deeply indebted to many people for their assistance in the writing and illustrating of this History. In particular, I would like to thank Frank Jessup for his unfailing interest, help, encouragement, and advice. I am grateful to him, and to a former colleague, Dr. Janet Cooper, Assistant Editor of the Victoria History of the County of Oxford, for their reading of the text and for their helpful comments. All its good points are theirs, its errors and short-comings are mine alone. I am also grateful to the Editor of the Victoria History for allowing me access to, as yet, unpublished material. My thanks are due to members of the staff of the Ashmolean Museum, the Bodleian Library, the Oxford City Library, the Oxford City and County Museum, and the University Library, Cambridge. My task has been made easier by the patience of my illustrator, Alison Crawford, who drew all the marginal drawings with such care and attention to detail, and to the cartographer, Roy Mole, who has brought order to the large number of complicated maps. All the typing was done for me by Dorothy Jessup with speed and accuracy and to her I am especially grateful for frequent help as baby-sitter. I have benefited to a large extent from the advice and experience of both Lord Darwen and Noel Osborne, Editorial Director of Phillimore.

I have throughout the compilation of this book had the constant support of a long-suffering and uncomplaining husband, who has helped with all the least interesting work with understanding. To him, and to our daughter, Caroline, I humbly, but with the utmost pleasure, dedicate this History.

MARY JESSUP

Cambridge, 1975

*St. Christopher
fresco, Horley
church*

I   Introducing the County

Oxfordshire straddles the imaginary boundary between southern England and the Midlands. It is predominantly a rural county, most of the land being of average or good quality. The rivers Thames and Cherwell form the only natural boundaries of any length. The Thames was an early and important means of transport and communication, especially with London. For the most part it flows through open meadow and pasture land, but from Goring to Pangbourne the river passes through a gap between the Berkshire Downs and the Chilterns and the sides of the valley are steep and well wooded in places. The river has many tributaries, especially in the northern part of the county, and the Cherwell which rises in Northamptonshire and joins the Thames below Oxford is the largest. Neither it, nor the others, are navigable except for punts or canoes.

Cottages at Oddington

Oxford, the county town, with a population of 112,070 in 1973, is the largest urban area. Famous for its University for over 800 years, it has in the last 50 years acquired renown of a different kind as the home of the Morris motor car. Banbury is next in size with a population of 30,270 and is expanding rapidly. Called 'the Gateway to the Midlands', it has good rail and road communications with most of the Midland conurbations, and its interests lie there rather than in Oxfordshire. South of Oxford there are few towns of any size. This has always been the less well-off part of the county. In 1334 Oxfordshire yielded about 38s. 10d. per square mile in taxes, more than any other English county. Bampton hundred—a fiscal and judicial division—paid nearly four times as much per square mile as Langtree and Binfield hundreds in the south. Even though these differences were gradually ironed out, the northern part of Oxfordshire has tended to continue to outstrip the south where Henley, the largest town, had a population of only 11,790 in 1973. From earliest times the people here and in the neighbourhood have looked towards London for their livelihood. Corn, malt, wood, and dairy produce were sent there by river and more recently it has become a popular residential area for commuters travelling daily to London to work. This division in interests between the extreme north and south of the county has existed since the Anglo-Saxons first came to the region and is perhaps understandable when it is realised that Banbury is nearer to Birmingham and Henley to London than they are to each other.

13

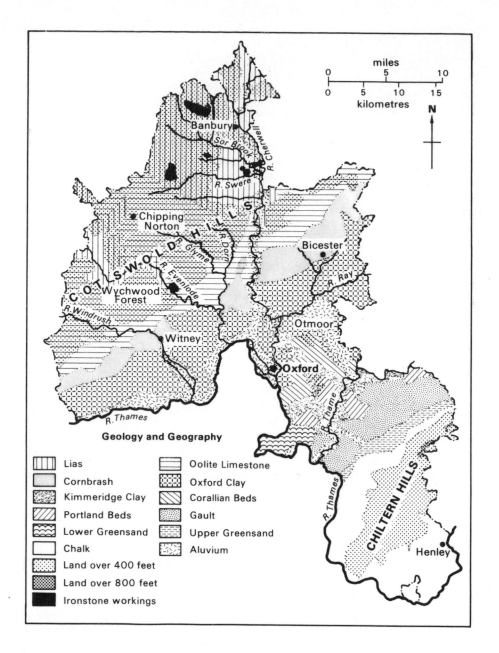

Geology and Geography

Lias	Oolite Limestone
Cornbrash	Oxford Clay
Kimmeridge Clay	Corallian Beds
Portland Beds	Gault
Lower Greensand	Upper Greensand
Chalk	Aluvium
Land over 400 feet	
Land over 800 feet	
Ironstone workings	

There is not much about Oxfordshire that is outstanding and little to set it apart from its five neighbouring counties. Within its boundaries it contains something of everything that is characteristic of this part of southern and midland England, but nothing that belongs to it alone. The geological formations which traverse Oxfordshire in a north-west to south-east direction all belong equally to, and are more conspicuous in, one or more of the surrounding counties. The Cotswolds which lie

14

across the north-western part of the county are at their best over the border in Gloucestershire but their influence in this part of Oxfordshire is extensive. In places the hills rise to over 700 feet, the fields are large and sheep were once a far more familiar sight than they are today. Whole towns and villages, as well as the field walls, are built of the grey limestone which characterises the Cotswolds, and comes from local quarries. The Cotswold wool trade brought prosperity to places like Witney, Burford, and Chipping Norton in the 14th and subsequent centuries, though never on the same scale as in Gloucestershire. Before weaving became concentrated in factories at Witney and Chipping Norton there were few cottages without a loom or spinning wheel.

Baptist chapel, Cote, 1664

Towards the extreme north of the county the limestone turns to a golden brown for here there are iron deposits. The unsightly remains of surface mining for the ore are scattered around Wroxton, Bloxham, and Hook Norton. Local quarries have produced a golden brown stone used extensively in Banbury and neighbouring villages. The rich rust-coloured corn-producing land was described in 1809 by the agricultural expert Arthur Young as 'the glory of the County, and adapted to every plant that can be trusted to it'.

Between the rivers Evenlode and Windrush there are still traces of the one-time royal forest which extended from Burford through Wychwood, Charlbury, Woodstock, Stowood, Shotover, right across to Bernewood in Buckinghamshire. Here many kings of England followed the chase and hunting rights were jealously guarded. At varying times Burford, Bampton, Bicester, and Woodstock were famous for the manufacture of leather riding gear. The forest was gradually cleared and finally enclosed in the mid-19th century leaving only 1,500 acres of Wychwood Forest as a reminder.

Although the region south of the cornbrash—a type of rubbly lime-stone especially good for wheat—as far as the foothills of the Chilterns appears to form one vast plain, it is in fact broken by the Oxford Heights. They lie across the narrowest part of the county and rise to 562 feet at Shotover. Over the border in Berkshire, Cumnor and Boars Hill are part of the same formation. Place-names like Stanton (farm on stony ground) and Stowood (stony wood) indicate the line of the outcrop. The Corallian and Portland beds have been extensively quarried for use in Oxford and neighbouring villages. Much of the clay which forms the basis of the plain, and which provided the materials for making bricks, is overlain by gravel and alluvium deposits. The gravels attracted some of the earliest settlers in the county for the land was light to work and well-drained. Now the gravels around Standlake, Yarnton, Cassington, and Dorchester* and Benson are

15

Estate cottages, Stonor

being extracted for building and road-making materials. As a whole, the plain is well-treed with much meadow and pasture land. One unusual feature is Otmoor, once a large marsh covering 4,000 acres, but now drained. Much of the land alongside the Thames and Thame is low lying and liable to flood in wet weather. The villages and towns in the southern part of this plain are built mainly of brick and, near the Chilterns, of flint. The flint comes from outcrops on the Chilterns which begin in Oxfordshire but reach their maximum development in Buckinghamshire. In places the range rises to over 800 feet and has the appearance of a formidable barrier. The scarp is treeless, the fields at the bottom featureless and pale in colour from the chalk. At Chinnor the chalk is utilised in a cement and lime works. The dip slope is thick with beechwood which once supported a thriving hand-made furniture industry based at High Wycombe.

This neat, extensively cultivated and tamed landscape, the work of generations of men and women, took thousands of years to achieve and it is still being altered to meet man's present and future needs. What each generation has contributed will become clearer, it is hoped, as the history of the county is unfolded.

*All references to Dorchester in this book are concerned with Dorchester-on-Thames, Oxfordshire, and should not be confused with Dorchester, Dorset.

1. Foxley Farm, Eynsham. The cropmarks indicate the presence of round barrows, ring ditches, an Iron Age settlement, trackways and enclosures.

2. The Rollright stone circle, consisting of over 70 monoliths, was probably constructed by the Beaker Folk.

3. Madmarston Iron Age hill fort, occupied from 200 B.C. to 50 A.D., was defended by three banks and a ditch, now much reduced by ploughing.

4. Stonesfield. The lower panel of the 4th-century Roman pavement depicts Bacchus riding the panther. It was found in 1712 and destroyed.

II Early Settlers

Most of the region which became Oxfordshire was covered with thick forest when the first people arrived there. These folk, who lived by hunting, were attracted by an abundance of game and fish and by a ready supply of flint in the Chilterns for fashioning into tools. A few hand-axes made by these Palæolithic or Old Stone Age people have been found in the gravels between Summertown and Radley, around Ewelme and Ipsden, and between Caversham and Henley. In the Mesolithic or Middle Stone Age, people living on the slopes of the Chilterns, sometimes called the Forest Folk, were making large and heavy tools, while in the region between the rivers Evenlode and Cherwell men used smaller and lighter ones.

Palæolithic hand axe, Dorchester

Sometime before 3,000 B.C. a revolutionary way of life was introduced by newcomers from the Continent. These folk, who heralded the Neolithic or New Stone Age, were much more sophisticated. They knew how to make pottery, used bone, stone, and wood, as well as flint for tools, grew corn and kept animals, built long barrows in which their dead were interred, and constructed the earliest henge monuments. Their long barrow at Ascott-under-Wychwood had a false entrance—perhaps to mislead would-be grave robbers—and under the large mound several bodies were buried in stone cists. Around Stanton Harcourt, Eynsham, and Cassington the light, well-drained soils especially suited the primitive farmers. They cleared the ground by burning and then sowed corn and other cereals. Some of the men may have been herdsmen who grazed their sheep and oxen on the meadowlands by the rivers in summer and on the uplands when the ground was flooded. They dug numerous pits for storing corn and when no longer needed filled them up with domestic rubbish. Their huts were flimsy structures which have left no discernable traces. Through this part of Oxfordshire ran a route to North Wales and the Lake District along which stone axes were traded. Other Neolithic farmers lived around the Dorchester area where many of their earthworks and cremation burials have been located. The ashes of the dead were put into holes in the ground dug so as to make a circle of burials. Ditches and banks were constructed around the burials to demarcate the area of the cemetery. Several of these cemeteries were found a mile north-north-west of Dorchester. Associated with the cemeteries was a simple form of

17

Beaker, North Stoke

henge monument. Thirteen holes varying greatly in size—the largest measuring 15 feet by 3 feet 6 inches and the smallest 4 feet by 2 feet 6 inches—were dug in an irregular circle surrounded by two ditches, one oval and one square. No trace was found of any wooden or stone uprights that might once have stood in the holes, and the archæologists consider it to have been a sacred site used for now unknown rituals.

Towards the close of the Neolithic period (about 2,000-1,500 B.C.) the Beaker folk, named from their distinctive beaker-shaped pots, came to Britain from the Rhineland and Low Countries. They, too, were attracted to the Stanton Harcourt and Dorchester areas and appear to have mixed amicably with the Neolithic folk.

They constructed numerous low mounds each surrounded by a circular or ring ditch. Many of these structures contained no remains to indicate to what use they were put. Sometimes, however, one or more of the Beaker folk have been found under the mounds buried in deep pits together with their pottery. At Dorchester one young man was interred with two small copper knives and a stone wrist-guard.

The Beaker folk were an active, vigorous people. They probably constructed the henge monument known as the Devil's Quoits near Stanton Harcourt. Several large monoliths were set up standing in a circle surrounded by an immense ditch and bank. One of the stones was taken away about 1680 by a local farmer to make a bridge, and in 1942 when part of the site was excavated, all but one of the stones had been removed from their original settings. At Rollright, the Beaker folk seem to have been responsible for constructing the large stone circle of over 70 monoliths. Local legend has it that they are a king and his men who were turned to stone by a witch and who come alive at night. What these henges were for remains a mystery.

The Beaker folk also took a leading part in encouraging trade in metal goods between the Oxfordshire region and Ireland. Bronze goods were never plentiful and were consequently greatly treasured. The cauldron found at Shipton-on-Cherwell was worn quite thin and had been repaired several times. Bronzesmiths travelled around the countryside gathering together broken or out-dated tools for casting anew. Occasionally they buried their hoards for safety and never retrieved them.

In the 6th century B.C. new ideas were once more infiltrating into the region with the introduction of iron tools. Iron ore, possibly extracted from the ironstone country of north Oxfordshire, was roasted in pits at Church Hanborough and iron currency bars were used at the Madmarston hill fort. Iron, like bronze, was never widely distributed at this time.

18

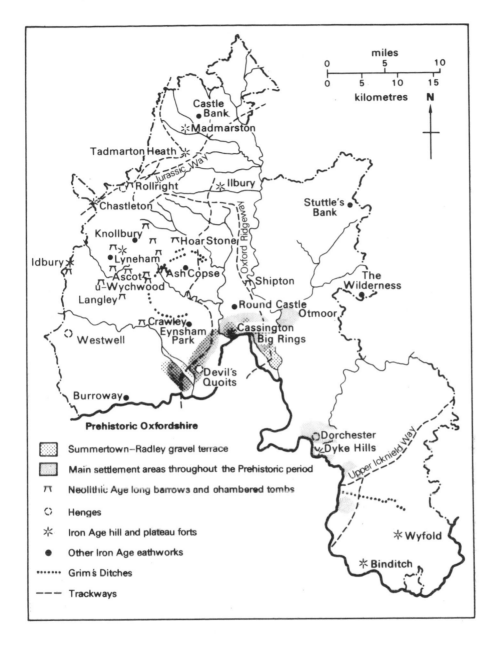

Prehistoric Oxfordshire

⬚	Summertown–Radley gravel terrace
▨	Main settlement areas throughout the Prehistoric period
⊓	Neolithic Age long barrows and chambered tombs
◌	Henges
✳	Iron Age hill and plateau forts
●	Other Iron Age earthworks
·······	Grim's Ditches
---	Trackways

The population of the Oxfordshire region was on the increase and families now began to settle in parts of the county previously avoided. One such settlement was at Great Milton. Iron Age folk lived in small groups, sometimes of no more than one or two families. Their huts were round or rectangular and made of wooden supports, wattle and daub walls, and thatched roofs and stood inside ditched enclosures. Close by were numerous pits used for storing grain, water, and possibly

19

*Dobunnic coin,
North Leigh*

manure, and when disused filled with refuse. The outlines of their fields have been traced on air photographs and by excavation, and apart from growing cereals, they kept horses, some of which pulled carts, and oxen, pigs, sheep and goats. There were querns for grinding corn, and hay was dried on wooden racks. Loom weights and bone combs were part of their weaving equipment and hides were worked with scrapers, knives, and borers. Their dead were sometimes dumped in the infilling of rubbish pits.

Some of the Iron Age people joined together to build the hill and plateau forts which lie dotted about the county, as can be seen on the map. Some were only temporary refuges or stock enclosures and show little signs of occupation. But the hill fort at Madmarston was obviously a defensive site surrounded by three banks and a ditch, once a formidable barrier, now much reduced by ploughing. The fort was occupied for about 250 years (200 B.C.-50 A.D.) and may have been the centre of a local tribe.

During the 1st century B.C. the Catuvellauni, a Belgic people who had a large tribal capital at Camulodunum (later Colchester) began to infiltrate into parts of eastern Oxfordshire. Their pottery and coins were used by the inhabitants of a small settlement at Dorchester, and at Watlington a woman, perhaps the wife of a Belgic chieftain, was buried with four very fine wheel-made pots of a type found in great numbers at the Belgic capital. In the north of the county the Catuvellauni penetrated as far as the river Cherwell. On the western side of the river no one tribe was predominant, but the Dobunni, a British tribe based in Gloucestershire, held a certain amount of influence, and their coins were in use here. Before 50 A.D. Grim's Ditch, an earthen bank and ditch, was constructed between the rivers Windrush and Glyme enclosing an area of about 20 square miles. Why such a massive work was undertaken is not clear. Perhaps it was the local British tribes endeavouring to prevent the Catuvellauni from advancing further west. Or it may have been the work of the Catuvellauni and others trying to halt the progress of the Romans, who were then moving into that area bent on subduing the local population. The other Grim's Ditch, in the south of the county, was also constructed about this time. It does not seem to have had any military significance and may only be a boundary between two tribes with differing means of livelihood, one based on cultivation and sheep, the other on pigs and cattle.

20

III   Roman Oxfordshire

The Romans came to Britain for the first time in 55 and 54 B.C., but their attempts then to conquer the country failed. They returned in 43 A.D., landing in Kent, and this time they were successful in subduing opposition to their occupation. It took them only four years to cross southern Britain and establish a temporary western frontier along the line of the Fosse Way from Exeter to Lincoln. They reached this position by crossing north Oxfordshire from east to west, building as they went a road later called Akeman Street. When completed it connected the important centres of London, Verulamium, and Cirencester. The other major Roman road through the county ran north to south from Towcester to Silchester, passing through the two Roman Oxfordshire towns of Alchester and Dorchester. The roads were built to last, up to 25 feet wide in places, with brushwood foundations in wet areas like Otmoor, and paved with slabs of local stone or gravel bound with clay. Earlier trackways, including the Icknield Way in the south-east of the county and the Portway in the north, remained in use and were partly paved.

Romano-British altar, Dorchester

Alchester and Dorchester—their Roman names are lost—had no known military significance, though Alchester may have served as a supply depot for Roman troops serving in the west. Alchester was intended to defend a road junction and Dorchester a river crossing, but they were also tax-collecting, police, posting, and market centres for their respective neighbourhoods. In the early part of the 3rd century one important official responsible for collecting taxes in kind for the army was resident in Dorchester. He erected an altar there which when found in 1731 was inscribed 'I(ovi) O(ptimus) M(aximo) et Numinib(us) Aug(ustis) M(arcus) Vatr(ius) Severus B(eneficiarius) Co(nsulari)s Aram Cum Cancellis d(e) S(uo) P(osuit)' (i.e., Marcus Vatrius Severus a *beneficiarius consularis* set up at his own expense this altar and its railings to Jupiter Optimus Maximus and the Deity of the Emperor). The altar was sold for a guinea shortly after it was found, and in 1913 was in the gardens of Broome Park, near Canterbury, but it was then given away and its whereabouts are now unknown.

Occupation of Alchester started about 50 A.D. and it probably superseded an earlier fort at Little Chesterton. It covered 25 acres enclosed by a ditch and rampart. At first people lived in timber houses or wattle and daub huts, and because it was low-lying and

21

damp they had to raise the ground level and dig drainage ditches to prevent their homes from being flooded. About 125 A.D. the defences were improved by the addition of a stone wall with two or more corner towers. Buildings were rebuilt in stone, and there was at least one of importance near the centre of the town, though its function is unknown. The layout of the streets was partly changed in the late 2nd and 3rd centuries when a road was built where there had once been a house. Unfortunately, the removal of stone and constant ploughing of the site by later generations have obliterated the 4th-century buildings and it is only possible to tell from coins and pottery finds that there was no significant decline in the intensity of occupation during that century.

Roman Dorchester, which covered 13½ acres, was established later than Alchester, probably about 70 A.D., and superseded or was set alongside the Belgic settlement. The earliest buildings were timber-framed with clay floors. A 1st-century defensive ditch was reinforced by a rampart about 185 A.D. and 100 years later a wall was added. Finally in about 360 A.D. external towers were built. A road ran through the fort on a north-south alignment connecting up with the main Roman road from Silchester to Towcester. A few of the later houses have been identified; a 3rd-century building contained kilns, ovens, and hearths. Both towns had cemeteries outside their walls.

Though both were thriving communities employed mainly in trade and the care of travellers, they remained small settlements with populations of only a few hundred each, unsophisticated and lacking the facilities and amenities of the larger Roman towns.

Town life was for the few and most of the people in Oxfordshire were occupied working the land. For many this meant little change in their way of life from what it had been before Britain became a province of the Roman Empire. There were several small, poor communities cultivating the lighter land especially in the region around Cassington and Standlake, along the Thames gravels, and around Dorchester. They lived in wattle and daub huts, had few metal implements or ornaments and the prized Samian ware was rarely found in their settlements. On the other hand in the north of the county, particularly along the line of Akeman Street west of the Cherwell, there were great changes during the Roman period. Here the more progressive and wealthier of the Dobunni and Catuvellauni farmed the heavier soils which had so far been left largely uncultivated. It was excellent corn-producing land and they took advantage of the demand for food for the army. Here also were the first, and later the more pretentious, of the villas or country estates in the county. The

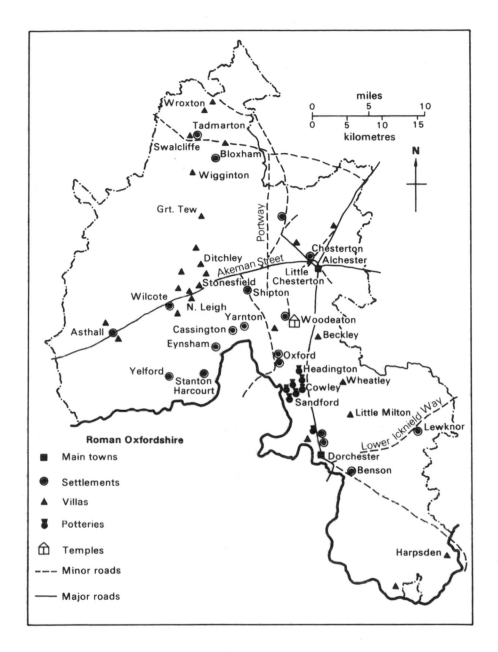

Roman Oxfordshire

■   Main towns

●   Settlements

▲   Villas

⬗   Potteries

⌂   Temples

---   Minor roads

—   Major roads

villas were not confined to this region, but in southern Oxfordshire they were smaller—Beckley never progressed beyond four rooms, and the larger villas like that at Harpsden near Henley were occupied by people of no great standing.

The northern group of villas also varied in size and style but on the whole were more highly developed. The villa at North Leigh had a long and complicated history, finally becoming one of the largest

23

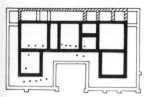

Ditchley villa: four phases of growth

of its kind in Britain. The first villas were very modest timber buildings, probably like barns to look at, and doubling the functions of home and cattle-shed. In the 2nd century many were rebuilt in stone on more ambitious lines reflecting their owners' success in farming. The timber house at Ditchley, built about 70–80 A.D., was replaced by a rectangular range of rooms with two projecting wings comprising entrance hall, dining-room, main living-room, kitchens, bedrooms, and baths. Though this was a vast improvement on the earlier building, the accommodation remained at the level of a comfortable farmhouse. Facing it from the other end of the enclosure was a large timber building which must have housed the slaves who worked the land. The villa was partly destroyed by fire about 200 A.D. and left to decay for at least 100 years. When it was rebuilt early in the 4th century, it had two storeys and a colonnaded entrance. The roof was tiled with slates of the Stonesfield type, the windows glazed, the walls decorated, and tesserae must have at one time been laid in the pink mortar floors, but there was no heating system nor any baths. In place of the slaves' quarters a stone granary estimated to have held the produce of 1,000 acres was built, and a new threshing floor was laid out where the corn was spread for the animals to tread the ears. The estate was now worked by labourers living outside the villa enclosure. At North Leigh also there was much reconstruction; the final house had a dining-room with heated walls, painted with panels enclosing olive branches, and a vaulted ceiling, elaborate baths, and fine pavements in three colours. At Wilcote the 4th-century villa had over 20 rooms placed around a central courtyard, a bath suite, a granary, and what appears to have been an underfloor heating system for drying grain. At Stonesfield the 4th-century villa had very elegant pavements. One, depicting Bacchus and the panther, was found in 1712 during the course of ploughing, but arguments between the landlord and tenant of the site about sharing the profits of showing it to the public led to its destruction by the tenant who 'maliciously tore it to pieces'. In 1779-80 two geometric pavements were exposed, but at the time of enclosure in the 19th century the site was divided between three proprietors and the pavements were gradually destroyed by ploughing.

There were no minerals to interest the Romans—they do not seem to have worked the ironstone in the north of the county, and though local stone was used for building and in road construction, no Roman quarry has been identified. Sizeable communities of potters grew up close to the Roman road between Dorchester and Headington. A pottery at Cowley was in production by the end of the 1st century A.D. It was a successful venture to judge from the rough stone hut floors,

24

habitation refuse, kiln, puddling hole, and waste dumps, and it remained in use until shortly after 340 A.D. Other successful potteries were at Rose Hill, Oxford, and on the site of the Churchill Hospital where *mortaria,* or mortars, for pounding food, were made in at least four kilns. At Sandford-on-Thames large quantities of imitation Samian ware were made during the 3rd and 4th centuries. No kiln has been found more than two miles from the road, which must have greatly facilitated trade, but it is not known how far afield the pottery was sent.

Statuette from Woodeaton temple

The Romans introduced their own religions to Britain, but tolerated and even influenced the worship of local deities. Iron Age people may have considered Woodeaton a sacred place before the first Romano-British temple was built there towards the end of the 1st century A.D. Many of the objects found associated with the building belonged to Iron Age folk and there are signs of intensive occupation by them of the surrounding area. The cult is unknown although the number of model axes found on the site suggests a god and the model birds indicate a goddess. The many coins found around the entrance to the temple may have been gifts to the deity or perhaps were dropped by pilgrims purchasing ornaments, model tools, or figurines offered for sale at a festival or fair connected with the cult. The temple was rebuilt and enlarged about 150 A.D., and was in use up to and possibly beyond the Roman withdrawal from Britain.

During the latter part of the 4th century barbarian raids on Britain and other parts of the Roman Empire were seriously undermining Roman authority and control. The Picts and Scots were attacking in northern Britain and Hadrian's Wall was abandoned in 383 A.D. Coastal defences failed to keep out the Saxon raiders. The Empire had to withdraw its men about 425 A.D. to defend continental possessions and finally Rome itself. The effects were disastrous and led to the gradual breakdown of all the civilising influences associated with Roman Britain. Life in the villas slowly decayed. Parts of the North Leigh villa were destroyed by fire after it had been used as a barn, or perhaps by squatters. At Ditchley the roof collapsed, the slates lying where they fell. Between the departure of the owner and its final abandonment early in the 5th century, estate officials or maybe squatters again camped in the house, lighting fires on the floor of one of the rooms. The concern felt about the breakdown of law and order led to the burial between 395 and 410 A.D. of a hoard of over 1,000 coins at Kiddington, half a mile from the Ditchley villa. The roads fell into disrepair and then into disuse. Only the stretches between Bicester and Towcester and east of Bicester towards Aylesbury have survived as major roads. The first of these is recorded in the place-name of Stratton (street) Audley where the Roman road later formed part of the parish boundary.

Alchester which as a settlement had no natural advantages, was abandoned soon after the Roman withdrawal. At Dorchester, however, it was a different matter. Here some sort of town life was to continue and flourish anew under the Anglo-Saxons.

IV The Anglo-Saxon Conquest and Settlement

Dorchester, unlike Alchester, had grown up in an area which had long attracted settlers. Under Roman rule it must have played an important part in the administration of the surrounding region. When the Romans themselves withdrew, mercenaries from among the Anglo-Saxon tribes of north-west Europe—the very same people who were raiding the south and east coasts of Britain—were enlisted by the Romans and sent to Dorchester to garrison the town and maintain some semblance of order. They arrived towards the end of the 4th century and some of their graves have been found nearby. Others may have been sent to the Romano-British Thames-side villages in an attempt to keep control of the area. When the Anglo-Saxon invasion of Britain was well under way in the 5th century those who penetrated into south Oxfordshire settled in Dorchester, where Saxon huts overlie the Romano-British buildings, and in the neighbouring villages. Many of these people probably came from East Anglia along the Icknield Way or up the Thames. In 571 Cuthwulf won Benson and Eynsham from the native British inhabitants for his brother Ceawlin, King of the Gwissae, a Saxon tribe. Ceawlin's father, Cerdic, had landed near Portsmouth in about 495 and had steadily won his way north. Further successes followed for Ceawlin and his people at the battle of Fethanleag, probably Stoke Lyne, in 584, when the Gwissae captured many villages. Cuthwulf was killed during the fighting and may have been buried under a large barrow at Cutteslowe destroyed in 1261 by order of the sheriff because it had become a meeting-place for robbers. Other victories in Hampshire, Wiltshire, Somerset, and Berkshire enabled Ceawlin and his successors to establish the kingdom of Wessex, which included much of southern Oxfordshire.

In the north of the county the Anglo-Saxons arrived mainly in the 6th and 7th centuries. Some came up the Thames and its tributaries; others were members of the Hwicce, an Anglian tribe, who gave their name to Wychwood Forest and whose territory included Gloucestershire, Warwickshire, and Worcestershire. But most came from the kingdom of Mercia which was based on the upper reaches of the river Trent and it was the Mercians who gained control of most of north Oxfordshire.

Apart from the battles that the Gwissae fought, there were numerous skirmishes between the invaders and the invaded, especially at river

Brooch, Dyke Hills burials

27

Anglo-Saxon Oxfordshire

R.Thames British river & place-names

- ●   Early English place-names
- ◉   Pagan cemeteries & settlements
- *   Pagan barrow & princely burials
- ✝   Churches with Saxon architecture
- ▉   Churches known from documentary evidence
- ⌂   Early monasteries or minsters
- ▉ **Bloxham**   Villae Regales–Royal Estates
- ⅄   Battles
- ▨   Taken into Oxfordshire 1844–1896
- ▢   Taken out of Oxfordshire 1844–1911

crossings, where swords and other weapons have been found. Looting must have been widespread. Ceawlin captured 'countless spoils' after the battle of Fethanleag and brooches and pottery, once the property of the British, turn up in the invaders' graves. There is no reason, however, for supposing that the British were massacred wholesale as once was thought, even though there are only two settlements in Oxfordshire which have preserved their British names. They are

28

Walcot which means 'cottages of the serfs'—doubtless some of the native population became the slaves of the Anglo-Saxons—and Dorchester which takes it name from Doricicon, a British word and ceaster, a Roman fortified place.

Anglo-Saxon crucifix, Langford church

Dorchester stood out as an important and flourishing community during the early 7th century and was probably a royal stronghold of the kings of Wessex when Bishop Birinus arrived from Rome in 634. He had been sent by the Pope to the Midlands, but finding the people of Wessex still 'completely heathen' set about converting them to Christianity. He baptised King Cynegils and Dorchester became his episcopal see. Although he 'built and dedicated several churches and brought many people to God' the extent of his success in Oxfordshire must have been limited by the division of the area between two rival kingdoms and by the refusal of the king's son, Cenwalh, to be baptised, for his mission depended on royal support. Cenwalh, who was eventually baptised while temporarily exiled from Wessex, founded another bishopric after he became king, with a Saxon bishop, at Winchester. He had grown tired of the 'foreign speech' of Agilbert, the second Bishop of Dorchester, who had been born in France. Agilbert was furious with the king for his high-handed action and withdrew to the Continent, leaving the Dorchester see vacant.

In the north of the county, the first Bishop of the Mercians, Diuma, may have been buried at Charlbury in 658. Owing to the successes of the kings of Mercia against the kings of Wessex, Dorchester was in the hands of the Mercians between 675 and 685, and the vacant bishopric was then filled by a Mercian bishop. This bishop acquired a very large estate in the Banbury region and Banbury itself probably had an early and important church of which there is now no trace. There were no more bishops of Dorchester, except briefly in about 737, until 886, when the bishop of Leicester, into whose diocese Oxfordshire had been absorbed, moved from Leicester to Dorchester for safety from Danish raiders. The bishops remained in Dorchester until the Norman Conquest, the see extending as far north as the river Humber.

Oxfordshire remained divided between Wessex and Mercia for several hundred years during which time much fighting took place between the two, each seeking to establish a supremacy over the other. But in the late 9th century both were threatened by an outside force —the Danes—and instead of fighting each other they had to concentrate their efforts on keeping back a common enemy. In 911-912 King Edward the Elder laid out the boundaries of Oxfordshire and other shires in central England as part of a defensive organisation directed against the Danes. Oxford is referred to for the first time, although

*An Anglo-Saxon
ploughman*

there had been a settlement there for over 100 years, but it was not until 1010 that the county was mentioned by name. The county was not safe from the Danish raiders—in 914 Hook Norton was ravaged by a Danish army and many men were slain, and in 1009 they attacked and set fire to Oxford. Horse trappings found in the river Cherwell below Magdalen Bridge, Oxford, and in the river Ray at Islip, belonged to these and similar raiding parties. Gradually, however, English supremacy was established over the Danes, and peace restored to England.

What was it like to live in Oxfordshire between the time its boundaries were laid out and the Norman Conquest of 1066, a period of less than 150 years?

The county was no longer disputed territory between two warring peoples, but part of the larger kingdom of England. The king had seven major royal estates in Oxfordshire, centred on the villages of Bampton, Bloxham, Benson, Headington, Kirtlington, Shipton-under-Wychwood, and Wootton. From them the surrounding countryside was administered and here the king's rents in kind—corn being the most important—were received. He had a residence at Kirtlington where a royal council met in 977, and probably another on the Headington estate. There was a royal hunting lodge at Woodstock, and Edward the Confessor, the last of the Anglo-Saxon kings of England, was born at Islip and hunted in the Forest of Wychwood. Royal councils met at Oxford and Edward was there in 1065, shortly before his death, to negotiate peace with rebels from Northumbria.

The rest of the land was held from the king by the church—the bishop of Dorchester held large estates—and by leading laymen. The land was worked by peasants probably on the open-field system. Life was hard and tedious for the peasant. Ælfric, the first Abbot of Eynsham, wrote of their daily lives about the year 1,000. The ploughman's day was especially onerous. He went out at daybreak, drove the oxen to the field and yoked them to the plough. Every day he had to plough a full acre or more. He had a boy to urge on the oxen with a goad. He had to fill the oxen's bins, water them, and clean out their stalls. For the king's huntsman, however, there were rewards for good service—clothes, food, and an occasional horse or ring.

For most men there was little alternative work to cultivating the fields, for most settlements were self-supporting. Pottery and weaving were domestic crafts. A very high standard of craftsmanship was achieved in metal work and jewellery. The Minster Lovell jewel, so called because it was found there about 1860, is exceptional. It is constructed of gold and bears on one side a design in green, blue, and white enamel depicting a four-pointed star and a round-armed Anglian cross. It was probably made either at Winchester or Glastonbury in the same workshop as the Alfred jewel, which was found in Somerset.

The first Anglo-Saxon settlers cultivated the already popular lighter soils, but as the population grew new areas were cleared from waste and woodland. The pattern of settlement, familiar today, was already apparent in 1066. Villages were small, sometimes no more than a few families. Only Oxford could in any sense be called a town. People lived in wattle and daub huts with thatched roofs or in larger rectangular timber buildings—styles of construction that had been in use for hundreds of years. Just how many villages had a church is not known, for most were built of timber of which all trace has long since vanished. In a few places just before the Conquest builders started to use stone, and some of their work can be seen at Langford, Caversfield, North Leigh, Waterperry, Swalcliffe, and Oxford.

This was Oxfordshire on the eve of the Norman Conquest; the people now living relatively peaceful, if hard, lives. This was not to last. Once more the native population was to be subjected to foreign invaders.

Minster Lovell jewel

31

V Rural Life in Medieval Oxfordshire

*Edward the Confessor
silver penny*

According to the Normans, Edward the Confessor had recognised William, Duke of Normandy, as his heir to the English throne in 1051-2, but when Edward died early in 1066, Harold, son of the deceased magnate, Earl Godwine, supported by the English, challenged his claim. The two met in battle at Hastings where Harold was killed. William marched to secure London by a round-about route which took him to Wallingford. Here he stayed the night while his troops camped on the other side of the river Thames in Oxfordshire. Next day they advanced eastwards across the southern tip of the county along the Icknield Way.

The Conquest brought disruption and people feared for their lives. The monks at Eynsham fled from the abbey; property and land values fell; and men perished in battle. William took various steps to secure his position and prevent further panic. He appointed Robert d'Oilly, a Norman, as sheriff of Oxfordshire and his chief representative in the county. d'Oilly saw to the building of a motte and bailey castle at Oxford where he was the first castellan. All manner of stories, some doubtless a distortion of the truth, spread about his harsh treatment of the local people. However, he married an English girl, though this may have been to gain access to her wealth. When in 1067, Wulfwig, the English Bishop of Dorchester died, William took the opportunity to appoint a Norman, Remigius, to the see. A few years later the bishopric was transferred from Dorchester 'where it had been founded of old without convenience or adequate dignity' to Lincoln. Dorchester, which had once been so important, sank into obscurity.

William's compatriots were rewarded for their loyalty and help with grants of land, once the property of Englishmen, to be held of him as his tenants-in-chief. This ensured that the influence of his supporters was widespread and lessened the likelihood of local opposition. It turned out to be the most far-reaching of the new king's actions in the county. In 1085 the king decided at one of his councils to find out 'what or how much each man had who was a holder of land in England, in land, or in cattle, and how much money it were worth'. The information that was gathered became known as the Domesday Book and in it is revealed the extent of the Norman holdings in Oxfordshire only 20 years after the Conquest. The king

32

5. Strip lynchets and ridge and furrow to the north of Shenington,
dating from the time of open-field farming.

6. The ruins of the 15th-century manor house of Minster Lovell, the home of the Lovell family
from about 1124 to 1602. The dovecote was part of the farm buildings. The church is built in
the cruciform Perpendicular style.

7. *(above)* Iffley church from the south west. This, the finest example of Norman workmanship in the county, was built about 1175-82 by the St. Remy family.

8. *(left)* The west end of Bloxham church, showing the magnificent 14th-century tower and spire.

was the most important landholder in the county and received £418 in rent from the royal estates of his English predecessors. His forest included Shotover, Stowood, Cornbury, Woodstock, and Wychwood, and extended in all over some 51,000 acres, and he received annually from the county £10 for a hawk and £23 for hounds. After the king, Odo, Bishop of Bayeux, was the next most important landholder, but he was arrested, probably for inducing knights from all over England to join him in an attempt to win the papacy for himself by force, and he forfeited his estates in 1082. Some of his land went to Wadard, who is pictured on the Bayeux tapestry in William's company at Hastings. The bishop of Lincoln received much of the land that had belonged to the bishop of Dorchester, including Thame, Banbury, Cropredy, and Great Milton. Robert d'Oilly, the sheriff, also held sizeable estates. Just a few Englishmen kept their land. Turchil of Arden, whose main estates lay in Warwickshire, held land at Drayton, but Orgar, who had once had land in Berrick Salome, was reduced to being a sub-tenant of Milo Crispin, a Norman baron.

Hic est Wadard

The land which William distributed among his followers was predominantly farmland settled by small communities. Only Oxford and Bampton had markets in 1086, for most settlements were self-supporting. Salt had to be brought from Droitwich where both Rollright and Bampton had salt pans. Estates were known as *maneria* or manors, and the tenants-in-chief as their lords. Because the lords were important men and had manors in more than one county they often rented their land to tenants, keeping only a small part—the demesne—in their own hands. In their absence the manors were run by stewards, bailiffs, or reeves. Below the sub-tenants in the manorial hierarchy came the customary tenants or villeins and then the cottagers. The tenants lived in villages or hamlets scattered about the manor. On the especially large ones there might be several settlements, while some villages grew up within two or more manors.

The land within the manor included arable, which lay in two large open fields, woodland and waste, and meadowland. Rivers provided fish and the water to drive mills for grinding corn. The two arable fields were divided up into strips, each representing a day's ploughing of approximately one acre. A villein's holding was usually 15 or 30 acres. Each man's holding, whether he was the lord or a villein usually lay scattered about the fields, probably to ensure a fair share of good and bad land, a system of cultivation which seems to have grown up under the Anglo-Saxons. Only a few cottagers held land in the open fields. Generally they had small enclosures attached to their homes.

All tenants were expected to do some work for the lord for little or no payment. For the villeins these customary services were especially onerous—usually two and a half or three days a week had to be spent ploughing, harrowing, mowing, carting, and dung-spreading on the lord's demesne, while at harvest and other boon times extra work was required. Occasionally there were special rewards for good work. At Newington the mowers at haymaking were entitled to one of the lord's better sheep while those who tedded and raked the hay received a wheaten loaf and cheese. On some manors a few villeins worked for the lord full-time. The bishop of Lincoln required on his manor of Thame that two of his villeins should be his ploughmen, two should keep his cows, and one should make his ploughshares.

For some counties details were entered in Domesday Book of the number of animals kept on the manors, but this was not done for Oxfordshire. Most manors, however, had oxen and horses for ploughing, bees for honey, and pigs, cows, bulls, and sheep for meat, skins, milk, and wool. The woodland and waste provided rough pasturage, but once the harvest was gathered in and gleaning was over, stock were allowed into the open fields. Meadowland was very valuable and its use by tenants was strictly controlled, for the hay crop was the only reliable source of winter food for cattle.

The tenants had to attend the manorial court every few weeks where matters concerning the day-to-day running of the manor were heard. The lord had the right to raise taxes among his tenants, to take the best beast as heriot or death duty, and to exact fines on marriage or entry to land.

The manorial system remained in operation with few alterations until the outbreaks of the Black Death in 1349, 1361-2, and 1369. The effects of the disease were all the more far-reaching because during the preceding 250 years the population had been increasing and new land had been brought into cultivation to meet the demand for more food. Waste and woodland had been cleared and converted into arable, sometimes making a third open field as at Islip. On some manors the two fields were re-divided into three, thereby reducing from a half to a third the amount of land which had to lie fallow each year. Land cleared from woodland on the Witney manor amounted to 140 acres in 1283 and 696 acres by 1353. New settlements came into existence—Leafield in Wychwood was first mentioned in 1213, its name meaning an open space or clearing.

Just how many people died in the Black Death cannot be calculated, but about half the clergy perished, and on the Witney manor two-thirds of the villeins. The sharp reduction in population had immediate effects. Reclaimed land reverted to scrub. There was a shortage of labour and many villages were depopulated, though very few were completely deserted. In 1358 the lord of Tusmore turned the open

34

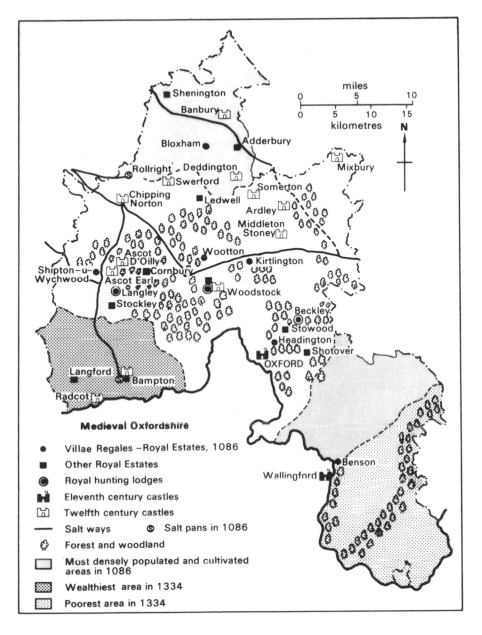

Medieval Oxfordshire

- ● Villae Regales – Royal Estates, 1086
- ■ Other Royal Estates
- ◉ Royal hunting lodges
- ⌂ Eleventh century castles
- ⌂ Twelfth century castles
- — Salt ways   ⑤ Salt pans in 1086
- ⌘ Forest and woodland
- ▢ Most densely populated and cultivated areas in 1086
- ▦ Wealthiest area in 1334
- ▦ Poorest area in 1334

fields into a park as all his labour force had died. In 1279 Tilgarsley had 52 tenants, but in 1359 it was said no one had lived there for nine years. A few villages revived later. In 1349-50 the water-mill at Steeple Barton was in ruins and 600 acres lay uncultivated. In 1353 the manor house was worth nothing, the dove-house was ruined and 1,200 acres were untenanted. A new village grew up about a mile away.

35

*Artist's impression
of Woodstock
manor house*

Many lords had difficulty replacing their dead tenants. At Witney in 1349 the manor court roll recorded that 'there is no one who wishes to take the land'. Many villeins took advantage of the demand for their labour and tried to obtain better working conditions. A few lords had already commuted some services for money before the Black Death, but now the process was accelerated. At Cuxham the villeins now paid up to 10*s.* a year for their holdings and the services were limited to a day each spent on hoeing and haymaking and two on harvest work each year. Attempts to reintroduce labour services failed in spite of tenants being offered 1*s.*, and the putting up of stocks to punish those who refused. Other villeins moved from manor to manor seeking the best conditions available, and at Cuxham in 1355 all vacant holdings had been filled by tenants from outside the manor. Some who stayed in the same place managed to build up sizeable holdings, renting more land as it fell vacant and hiring the less successful villeins to work for them.

For many of the lords it meant the end of demesne farming. Their profits had depended on cheap or free labour and this was no longer available. More and more demesne land was leased to tenants. By 1399 there was no arable demesne left on the Witney manor. Stock were retained, but in time the beasts were leased as well. Other tenants converted arable into pasture and increased their flocks of sheep for they required less labour and wool was profitable. Depopulation due to this change of land use became a matter for great concern. The 12 people evicted from Ledall in 1492 when 200 acres of arable were turned over to sheep were but a few of those who lost both their homes and livelihood during the latter part of the 15th century.

In spite of the ups and downs of rural life in the Middle Ages, Oxfordshire was very prosperous as a county. More and more markets were opened, and by the 14th century most places were within walking distance of at least one. Kings were frequent visitors to Woodstock, and for Henry I it was a 'favourite seat of his retirement and privacy'. He surrounded the hunting lodge there with a stone wall seven miles long, and was reputed to keep lions, lynxes, camels, and porcupines in the park. Henry II extended the forest to cover 102,400 acres, and Edward III built a hunting lodge at Beckley and King John another at Langley.

The county played little part in national affairs in the Middle Ages, but during the struggle between Stephen and Matilda for the crown Matilda occupied Oxford Castle in 1141-2, where she was besieged by Stephen. The story of her escaping at night across the frozen Thames, muffled in white clothes, is well-known. Several small castles were raised in Oxfordshire during this time, mainly by Matilda: Woodstock, Bampton, Deddington, Mixbury, and Middleton Stoney all belong to this period. They had short lives and were of little military significance. Only Banbury Castle, built by the bishop of Lincoln as the administrative centre of his large estate there, and Oxford Castle, survived the Middle Ages to play important parts in the Civil War of the 17th century.

VI Oxford, its Origins and Development

The Tower of St. Michael at the Northgate

People have been living in and around the site of the city of Oxford since at least 3,000 B.C. A much-used prehistoric trackway came down off the Berkshire Downs, forded the Thames at North (Ferry) Hinksey and made its way towards the Banbury region along the line of the modern Banbury Road. One after another, groups of Neolithic, Bronze Age, and Romano-British farmers settled close to it, especially around the University Parks and in parts of north Oxford.

Exactly when and how Oxford emerged as a town from these scattered dwellings is not clear. It may have started to grow after 727 A.D., the traditional date for the foundation in Oxford by St. Frideswide of a monastery or church in gratitude for her having been spared by divine intervention from an unwelcome suitor. People certainly lived in the southern part of St. Aldate's about 800, close to the conjectured site of the monastery and alongside a trackway which crossed the Thames at a ford where Grandpont was later built. Which of the two fords across the Thames gave Oxford its name is still debatable.

It was probably the Danish raids of the late 9th century that decided the kings of Wessex to turn the settlement into a fortified town. The site was naturally defended on three sides by the rivers Cherwell and Thames, and the southern tip of a gravel terrace which projected into the loop formed by the rivers provided a sound foundation on which to develop an administrative and defensive centre.

Oxford was planned with this in mind and it is reflected in the regular layout of the streets. The crossing of the four main axis streets of Cornmarket, St. Aldate's, High Street, and Queen Street, known for centuries as Carfax, formed the focal point.

The town was already well established when in 911-12 'King Edward succeeded to London and Oxford and to all the lands which belonged to them'. The early 10th-century ditch found beneath Church Street may be part of the town's first defences enclosing an area which extended from New Inn Hall Street to Catte Street. The town was enlarged and its safety improved by the addition of a rampart and palisade possibly in 912 and certainly long before the Norman Conquest. The line the defences then took was that of the medieval walled town.

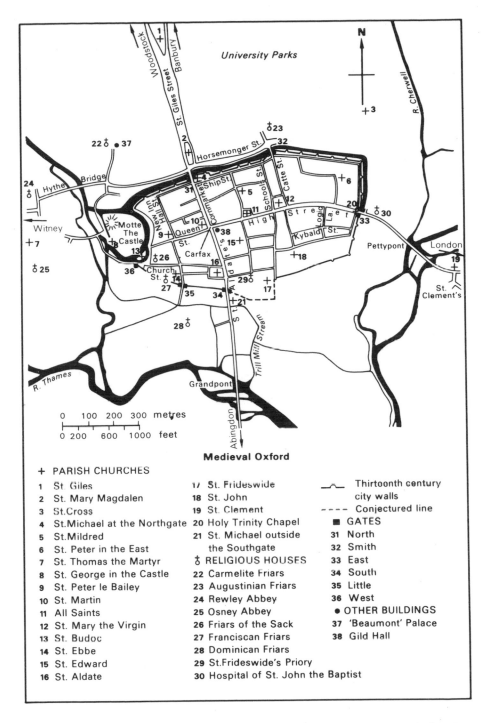

Medieval Oxford

+ PARISH CHURCHES

1 St. Giles
2 St. Mary Magdalen
3 St. Cross
4 St. Michael at the Northgate
5 St. Mildred
6 St. Peter in the East
7 St. Thomas the Martyr
8 St. George in the Castle
9 St. Peter le Bailey
10 St. Martin
11 All Saints
12 St. Mary the Virgin
13 St. Budoc
14 St. Ebbe
15 St. Edward
16 St. Aldate

17 St. Frideswide
18 St. John
19 St. Clement
20 Holy Trinity Chapel
21 St. Michael outside
   the Southgate

♱ RELIGIOUS HOUSES
22 Carmelite Friars
23 Augustinian Friars
24 Rewley Abbey
25 Osney Abbey
26 Friars of the Sack
27 Franciscan Friars
28 Dominican Friars
29 St. Frideswide's Priory
30 Hospital of St. John the Baptist

⌐⌐ Thirteenth century
    city walls
- - - Conjectured line
■ GATES
31 North
32 Smith
33 East
34 South
35 Little
36 West
● OTHER BUILDINGS
37 'Beaumont' Palace
38 Gild Hall

During the 10th and early 11th centuries Oxford flourished despite being attacked and burnt by the Danes in 1009. There were only

St. George's tower, Oxford Castle

two other places in England—London and York—with more moneyers than Oxford during Athelstan's reign (924-39). There must have been a market even though there is no mention of it until after 1086. Inhabitants made cloth and there were many leather workers living in Cornmarket. Houses were built of timber, wattle and daub and had long back yards or gardens where numerous rubbish pits were dug. The Saxon stone tower of the church of St. Michael at the Northgate, which still stands, was built about the time of the Conquest and there were several other churches. The town's central position in southern England was already very important. The first bridge over the Cherwell, Pettypont, was built by 1004 and greatly facilitated the passage of those attending the royal councils held in Oxford in the 11th century. The town was expanding beyond its defences into small suburbs. People lived east of the Cherwell in St. Clement's where late Saxon pottery has been found. In west Oxford people occupied the area between the defences and the river, and early in the 11th century Church Street was laid out to serve them. Others were building homes to the north of the defences where by 1074 the church of St. Mary Magdalen had been erected.

The years between 1066 and 1086 seem to have been disastrous for Oxford and for no explicable reason. It was one of the largest towns in England and in 1086 had a population of about 3,500 and between 900 and 1,000 houses, but over 400 of the houses were so decayed in 1086 that no taxes could be levied on the owners. The Norman sheriff, Robert d'Oilly, had made certain changes in the town but none can fully account for this. He superintended the building of a motte and bailey castle in west Oxford about 1071 which had meant the destruction of the small Saxon suburb and the realignment of the western defences. In 1074 he built the church of St. George in the Castle, the tower serving both as part of the defences and as the belfry. It and the crypt have both survived. d'Oilly also saw to the building of Grandpont, or Folly Bridge, which greatly improved communications with southern England.

Whatever had caused the decayed houses, by the early 12th century Oxford was once more flourishing. Much of its prosperity was due to the thriving market and trades. The right to make and sell goods in Oxford was jealously guarded by both the Gild Merchant and the trade gilds. In 1086 the burgesses of Oxford held Portmeadow, 500 acres to the north-west of the town, in common, and these men probably formed the original Gild Merchant to safeguard their interests. It was already well established in 1155 and was beginning to emerge as the chief governing body in the town. The Portmanmoot had then been in existence for at least 25 years. In 1155 the king

40

THE JESSE WINDOW IN DORCHESTER CHURCH, OXON.

9. The Jesse window in Dorchester Abbey church, dating from about 1340, and erected by the Augustinian canons.

10. The market place Watlington in 1824. The market hall, with a school-room over, were both erected by Thomas Stonor in 1664 and still stand.

11.   Thame High Street. A market has been held here since 1183-6. In 1221 the bishop of Lincoln 'made . . . an encroachment where he leased houses to increase his rent'— the Middle Row, which lies in the centre of the half-mile long street.

12.   Burford High Street, looking up the hill, in 1906. Once a busy coaching centre, it is now a favourite with tourists.

13. The Market House, Eynsham, in 1826. Eynsham belonged to the local abbey and first had a market in 1256.

14. Bicester. The Town House was erected by 1599 and it, together with the Shambles, was destroyed by rioters in 1826.

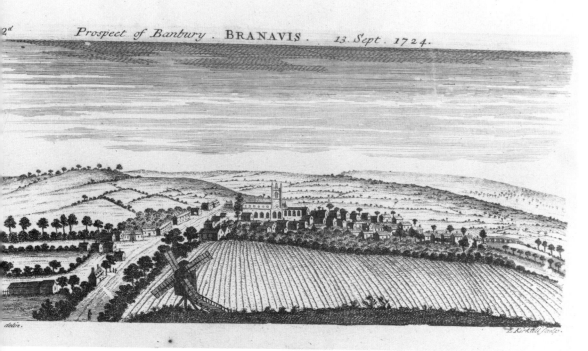

15.   Banbury from the south in 1724. The church of St. Mary was demolished in 1793 and rebuilt.

16.   Islip from the south east in 1822. Edward the Confessor was born here and later
gave the church to Westminster Abbey.

granted the burgesses a charter giving them the right to trade anywhere in England and Normandy free of all tolls and they were to enjoy the customs and privileges of the citizens of London. During the 13th century close trading contacts were established with London and Southampton and Oxford merchants attended fairs all over southern England. The burgesses were also given the privilege of assisting the king's butler at coronations and as only London and Winchester had similar functions to perform it indicates the importance of Oxford at that time. In 1191 the Gild was using a seal inscribed 'Sigill' Commune Omnium Civiu Civitatis Oxenefordie'—the Common Seal of all the Citizens of the City of Oxford. This is the earliest example of the use of such a seal in England.

Common seal of the City of Oxford

Of the trade gilds, the Weavers' was the oldest, formed before 1130, and the Corvesers soon after. Both introduced stringent regulations to protect their members from outside competition. No one was to practise the art of weaving within five leagues of Oxford and no one was to cut or sell leather in the town or suburbs unless he was a member of the respective gild. Everyone, however, could sell their goods in the weekly market. Sellers of straw, wood, furs, coal, rushes and brooms, bread, poultry, dairy goods, and pigs—to name but a few—all had their allotted places along both sides and in the middle of the four main streets. Cornmarket was widened in the 12th century to accommodate the sellers of corn who brought much of their produce to the wharf at Hythe Bridge. Horses were sold in Horsemonger Street, now Broad Street, and fish in Fish Street, now part of St. Aldate's. The Butter Bench stood at Carfax and the Butcher Row in Queen Street. Gild members were allowed to have permanent shops. Sometimes they were no bigger than six by ten feet, and were nearly all clustered in the streets around Carfax. Some gild members collected together according to their crafts, like the spicers and apothecaries along the north side of the High Street.

New buildings were frequently appearing, and some old ones were destroyed. Henry I initiated the building of a small royal residence at the west end of what became Beaumont Street. He and his successors stayed there from time to time and Richard I and John were born there. The hall was aisled and had a dais and gabled windows and the walls of the Queen's chapel were decorated with paintings of Biblical scenes. In 1308, however, Edward II allowed the sheriff to take timber and lead from the now dilapidated hall to repair the castle, and in 1318 he gave the palace to the Carmelite Friars.

After the Barons' War against John, the castle defences were strengthened and to do so St. Budoc's church was removed in 1216.

41

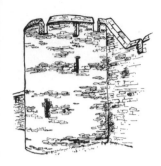

City wall

The earthen defences which surrounded the town were replaced by a large ditch and stone wall, part of which remains in New College gardens and between the backs of the houses in Ship Street and Broad Street. The gates into the town were impressive structures. By 1350 the wall had lost its significance and large parts of it were incorporated into houses and the ditch was filled in.

The town was steadily expanding throughout the 12th and 13th centuries. Kybald Street was laid out in 1130 and Logic Lane a little later. Tenements were divided up like those excavated in Cornmarket Street where one large property became three small shops with a larger tenement behind with a narrow street frontage. New people came to the town beginning with the foundation of the religious houses, then the first teachers and scholars, and finally the Friars. St. Frideswide's Priory was founded in 1122; seven years later came Osney Abbey which was established across the Thames from the castle. Rewley Abbey was opened in 1281 on what was later the site of the 19th-century L.M.S. station. The first scholars arrived towards the end of the 12th century and in 1221 attracted by this academic community, the Friars.

The arrival in Oxford of a community of scholars coincided with the rapid growth in the right of the Gild Merchant, citizens, and burgesses to run the town on their own. The town belonged to the Crown and in 1199 King John allowed the Gild Merchant and citizens to hold it as tenant-in-chief in return for the payment directly to the king, instead of through the sheriff, of the annual fee-farm rent of £63 0s. 5d. They were also to choose two bailiffs to collect the money. The first citizen to hold the office of mayor was Lawrence Kepeharme in about 1204. The mayor held a court on Fridays to deal with offences concerning the Gild and trade regulations, while freeholders, who were not members of the Gild, had to attend the Husting court on Mondays where matters concerning property were heard. In 1229 a new Gild Hall was acquired which stood on the site of all subsequent Town Halls. Before this the Gild had met in a house adjoining St. Martin's church and once in the churchyard itself. In 1295 the town sent representatives to Parliament for the first time.

The townsmen welcomed the influx of teachers and scholars. Students needed lodgings and were an easy prey for greedy landlords. But in 1192 the townsmen were complaining of the difficulties of providing enough food for so many students. By the early part of the 13th century there were about 1,500 students seeking accommodation from a population not much more than twice that number. Unscrupulous landlords let every room they could at inflated prices,

42

and to try and avoid bad feeling, a board of assessors was set up to settle fair rents. Food was expensive and often of poor quality. Complaints by members of the University grew in number and ferocity and rioting between students and townsmen was well organised and frequent. 'No sooner the bell rang a minute but they (the students) all left their meat, ran to their bows, swords, slings, bills, etc. and gathering together in a body fought most courageously against them (the townsmen) wounded many and made the rest fly'. Although Anthony Wood wrote this account in the 17th century it was probably a fit description of what was happening in earlier centuries.

Students were subject to ecclesiastical law, and punishments were usually more lenient than those meted out to laymen. The Chancellor of the University acquired extensive juridsiction over any case where a clerk was involved even when arrested by the town. Gradually the privileges and rights won by the citizens were whittled away; every time there was a serious riot, the town lost a privilege. After the St. Scholastica's Day fracas in 1355 in which townsmen and scholars were killed and maimed and much damage was done to property, the University was given complete control of the assizes of bread, ale, wine, weights and measures, and the Chancellor was given some jurisdiction over townsmen. The town was required to submit to an annual penance for its part in the riot and the mayor had to take an oath to uphold the liberties and privileges of the University.

15th-century shop

Not only did the town's privileges decline, but there was stagnation in trade and a fall in population. The weavers who had been doing so well in the 12th century and who numbered over 60, were reduced to a mere 15 after 1272 and in 1323 they were all said to be dead. The town suffered severely from the Black Death and in 1351 the townsmen complained that 'they are beyond measure impoverished by the pestilence and reckoned but feeble'. Empty and derelict houses within the walls were acquired by colleges and more and more of the town's centre was taken over for University purposes. In the suburbs houses lost their value and there was little or no new building. Some parishes were amalgamated and churches suppressed or absorbed into religious or collegiate foundations. In 1440 the citizens complained, probably somewhat exaggeratedly, that they were having difficulty raising the fee-farm and that taxes were too high because they had been fixed when the town was populous and now there was scarce a third of the laymen left and Oxford was mainly inhabited by scholars and their servants who were exempt from paying. More and more people were moving away. This unhappy state of affairs was to continue until the mid-16th century when once more prosperity returned to the town.

43

VII   The Medieval University

A Batchelor of Divinity, 1387

Oxford began to acquire a reputation as a place of learning during the early part of the 12th century. Theobald of Etamps called himself Master of Oxford and was lecturing in 1117 to over 60 students. About the same time, Walter, a scholarly man, was Archdeacon of Oxford and Provost of the College of Secular Canons of St. George in the Castle. Geoffrey of Monmouth, author of *The History of the Kings of Britain,* was a friend of his and possibly one of the canons. A little later Robert Pullen, a great theologian, lectured on the Bible, and in 1141 Robert of Cricklade, noted for his erudition, was Prior of St. Frideswide's Priory. Then about 1170 some of the English scholars ordered by Henry II to leave the University of Paris and return home, arrived to take up their studies in Oxford. In 1184 there was talk of a *studium generale* and Doctors of different faculties.

Masters and students alike seem to have been attracted to Oxford by its pleasant situation, by its central position in southern England, and by its remoteness from ecclesiastical control. The University was no more than a gild of teachers and scholars, who were all clerks by definition and who had combined together for mutual protection and convenience. As all education was under the control of the Church, a University in Oxford was subject to the authority of the bishop of Lincoln, who lived several days' journey away. In Oxford the University would be able to get on with the work of teaching and learning without too much interference from its spiritual superior.

This University bore no resemblance to its 20th-century namesake. There were no University buildings, colleges, administration, and few regulations, and it was by no means permanently established in Oxford. In 1209 when two clerics were hanged by the townsmen for a crime they had not committed the students left Oxford, some going to Cambridge. They did not return until 1214. In 1264 some students went to Northampton to avoid being caught up in the dispute between the king and Simon de Montfort. In 1334 half the scholars went to Stamford after serious rioting between rival student gangs, but the king ordered them to return to Oxford immediately. To safeguard against this happening again and the possibility of a rival University being set up, every M.A. had, until 1827, to take an oath not to teach at the pretended University of Stamford.

44

In spite of these upheavals the University grew rapidly in the 13th century. The Friars began arriving in 1221 and they greatly added to its size and reputation, for many of them were exceptionally learned men and excellent teachers. Roger Bacon taught theology and Robert Grosseteste, though not a Friar, taught for the Franciscans.

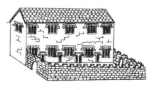

Old Arts School

Anybody could come to study in Oxford who was able to pay a master to teach him. Some of the students were only young boys and not all came to study seriously. The University tried, unsuccessfully, to insist that every scholar put his name on a master's roll (*Matricula*) and attend at least one lecture daily. A course of studies was laid down and supposed to be strictly followed, but there was no way of enforcing the regulations. The student studied grammar, rhetoric, and logic (the *trivium*), and arithmetic, geometry, astronomy, and music (the *quadrivium*). He attended lectures given by the Masters of Arts and learned to analyse and dispute. After four or five years he could 'determine' and become a Bachelor of Arts. Three years later he 'incepted' and became a Master of Arts and received a licence to teach. Six to eight years' further study were then required for degrees in Medicine, Civil and Canon Law, and Theology. No one could proceed to the study of theology until he had determined and incepted. It was this regulation that caused trouble between the University and the Friars, for the Friars were not allowed to pursue secular studies. However, the University reluctantly permitted the Friars to proceed direct to the study of theology by giving them graces. Later, relations between the two bodies deteriorated to such an extent that the University accused the Friars of preaching heresies and enticing young boys into their ranks.

Students, except the Friars and monks, lived in lodgings, but this was far from satisfactory. Discipline was lax and rents were high. In time halls or hostels were opened in ordinary houses and inns, leased by senior members of the University. The rooms were then let out to students. This system worked quite well and the University tried in 1414-20 to insist that all undergraduates should reside in a hall.

Some masters lectured to the students in the halls, but it was more usual for them to hire rooms as schools. Many of these belonged to local religious houses; in 1279 Osney Abbey owned about a tenth of all property in Oxford. Most of the Arts Schools were in Schools Street which ran from the west end of the church of St. Mary the Virgin northwards towards Broad Street. The Schools of Canon and Civil Law were clustered around the church of St. Edward. In 1439 the abbot of Osney replaced several of the Arts Schools owned by the abbey by a single new building which served as the main Arts School until the early 17th century.

45

Old Congregation House

It soon became necessary to provide for the government of such a large body and from 1214 a Chancellor was appointed to act as the representative in the University of the bishop of Lincoln. One of the first men to be appointed was Robert Grosseteste, who later became Bishop of Lincoln himself. He drew up regulations and arranged for the keeping of the University's sole source of income—an annual payment by the town of 52s. as a penance for hanging the innocent clerks in 1209. Later the Great Congregation or Convocation came into being to organise studies, finances, and litigation while Congregation was formed to cope with routine and minor matters.

University ceremonies and meetings took place in the church of St. Mary the Virgin. Then in about 1320 Thomas Cobham, Bishop of Worcester, built a Congregation House, with a small library above, on to the north side of the church. The first building planned and built by the University was the School of Theology or Divinity School, a very fine example of 15th-century vaulted work. Although the University suggested it about 1420, work did not begin until 1462, and financial difficulties and a shortage of labour delayed its completion until 1490. Over it was built a library named after Humphrey, Duke of Gloucester, its principal benefactor.

The first colleges began to appear during the second half of the 13th century. They were intended to provide a suitable atmosphere for graduates to study for higher degrees. Among the earliest was Merton endowed by Walter de Merton about 1263-4 for 11 graduates to study for their M.A.s. The exceptionally large chapel, and the library completed between 1373 and 1378, are its earliest surviving buildings.

It was not until William of Wykeham, Bishop of Winchester, founded New College in 1379 that the characteristic layout of all subsequent colleges was adopted. Wykeham had been Surveyor of the King's Works and he took a great interest in the buildings and the close association between the University and the Church explains his use of the monastic plan of quadrangles, cloisters, and chapel. His college, intended for 70 scholars from Winchester School, another of his foundations, was one of the largest then in Oxford and the first to provide for undergraduates. Magdalen College, founded in 1458, by William of Waynflete, Bishop of Winchester, copied this and accommodation for 30 'demies' between the ages of 12 and 25 years was planned.

The University's reputation as a place of learning was especially good in the 13th and 14th centuries. It produced many famous philosophers including Duns Scotus and William of Ockham, both Franciscan Friars. The heretical opinions of John Wycliffe, Master of Balliol, caused short-lived excitement, and Lincoln College was founded in 1427 by Richard Fleming, Bishop of Lincoln, to train a group of graduates

46

who could oppose the errors and heresies which were leading people astray. Famous among the astronomers were John Maudet, who compiled an astronomical table, and Richard Wallingford, who made an astronomical clock.

The 15th century was a period of regression reflecting the national disturbance caused by the Wars of the Roses, the failing state of the Church, and the unhealthy preoccupation of the colleges with lavish building plans. Discipline was lax and outbreaks of plague reduced the number of students to about 600 in 1450 compared with 3,000 in the 14th century, and many of the halls closed down. In 1523 the University complained that numbers were falling again because abbots were no longer sending their monks to be educated, and parents were unwilling to expose their sons to heretical ideas. In 1530 a committee was set up to examine heretical books, some of which were being sold at St. Frideswide's Fair in Oxford.

Lincoln College frontage

When the dissolution of the monasteries got under way, the University feared for its own future. However, only the monastic colleges were suppressed and far from suffering there was much to be won from the new order of things. Many colleges gained financially by grants of land and revenues formerly belonging to the religious houses. Cardinal College was founded in 1525, before the general suppression of the monasteries, by Thomas Wolsey, and was endowed with land and revenues worth £2,000 a year together with the site and buildings of the dissolved St. Frideswide's Priory. Wolsey embarked on making it the largest and most splendid of all the existing colleges. By 1529 the great kitchen, hall, and part of Tom Quad were completed, but then Wolsey fell from power. The college was re-established by the king as King Henry VIII's College in 1532 only to be suppressed and refounded by him in 1546 as Christ Church. He gave Christ Church the lands and revenues of Osney Abbey. The church of St. Frideswide's Priory became the college chapel, suitably shortened to fit in with Wolsey's grandiose building plans, as well as the cathedral church of the newly established diocese of Oxford, and the Dean became its principal.

The new ideas on doctrine and the break with Rome caused considerable upheaval and confusion in the University. It was unwillingly caught up in Henry VIII's attempt to legitimate his divorce from his first wife, the legality of which was debated in 1530 by a special University committee by order of the king. It gave an academically evasive reply.

By this time, however, the period of regression was over. There was the beginning of a revival in education, and the favours once shown to the monastic foundations came increasingly to be bestowed on the colleges leaving them strong and wealthy.

47

VIII   The Religious Life

William de Leicester,
Rector of Chinnor

The importance to men and women in the Middle Ages of their churches and the rites, festivals, and feasts connected with them cannot be over emphasised. Churches were rebuilt, enlarged, beautified, and adorned by successive generations of people, with a devotion and generosity seldom equalled in later times. The contemplative life with its demanding vows of chastity, poverty, and obedience, appealed strongly to men and women alike. They were eager not only to help found and endow monasteries and nunneries, but also to enter them and participate in an austere and simple life. However hard life might be, there was always the promise of eternal bliss.

There were some 180 churches in Oxfordshire in 1086 and by 1291 this number had grown to at least 260. Many were built by manorial lords alongside their homes or in the more populous parts of their estates. They regarded them as part of their property and claimed the right to a say in the appointment of clergy.

Before the Conquest many churches in the county were built of wood, but after 1066 stone became increasingly popular in north and central Oxfordshire and flint in the south. So much building and rebuilding took place during the 100 years following the Conquest that Norman architectural features are common. In some places even where restoration or complete rebuilding has obliterated all trace of Norman workmanship, the original font has been carefully preserved, as at Albury. The late 12th-century church at Iffley, built by a member of the St. Remy family to serve a parish created out of their manor, was fortunately left alone by later generations and is the most perfect example of a Norman church in the whole of Oxfordshire.

Other churches were not so fortunate and there are very few which are typical of a particular architectural style, although all are of interest. The largest and most splendid churches are to be found in north Oxfordshire where there was greater wealth than in the south. Money from the wool trade and farming was spent on enlarging and beautifying churches. The parish churches of Witney, Bampton, Chipping Norton, and Burford are all very fine buildings, but those at Bloxham and Adderbury are outstanding. Bloxham's splendour—the tower and spire are 198 feet high and the interior 110 feet long and 70 feet wide—is due to past royal patronage and rich lords. As it stands, the building is mainly of 14th-century Decorated style. At Adderbury the chancel and vestry were rebuilt between 1408 and

17.   Otmoor. This was transformed from marsh land into farm land after enclosure in the 19th century.

18.   Henley Bridge, 1791. In 1774 the wooden bridge was washed away in a flood and a new bridge, pictured here, was opened in 1786-7. The toll house stands in Berkshire.

19.   Ewelme grammar school founded in 1437 by the Duke and Duchess of Suffolk and now a primary school.

1419 in the Perpendicular style for about £400. The chief mason was Richard Winchcombe, who also built the Divinity School in Oxford and the beautiful Wilcote chapel in North Leigh church. Along the wall of the north aisle are carved a series of grotesque figures and musicians and their instruments.

In the south of the county by far the most interesting parish church is the abbey church of St. Peter and St. Paul, Dorchester. It probably stands on the site of the first church in the county—the Saxon cathedral founded in 634. Nothing remains of this building except for some stones in the north wall of the nave. After the Norman Conquest when the bishop moved to Lincoln, the church was handed over to secular canons and then in about 1140 to the Augustinian monks. It was they who rebuilt the church and provided many of the outstanding features for which the church is famous, among them the Jesse window, the only one of its kind to survive the dissolution of the monasteries. The local people were allowed to use part of the nave as their parish church and when the abbey was suppressed the chancel was purchased for them for £140.

Wilcote chapel, North Leigh

Any person of wealth could commemorate himself or his family by a gift to the church. At one time it was fashionable to erect a chapel as did Lady Elizabeth Blackett in about 1440 at North Leigh in memory of her first husband, Sir John Wilcote, their sons, and herself. Masses were said daily for all their souls. Some local dignitaries were commemorated in brasses. The oldest such brass in the county, made about 1320, is at Chinnor and is probably to the memory of William de Leicester, the rector. There are fine 15th- and 16th-century brasses in Thame church to the memory of the local influential families of Quatremaine and Dormer, while at Brightwell Baldwin a 15th-century brass, over eight feet long, commemorates the Chief Justice, Sir John Cottusmore, his wife, and 18 children. Elaborate tombs were put up in some churches, like the magnificent one for Alice, wife of William de la Pole, Duke of Suffolk, in Ewelme church.

The only instruction that the majority of people in the Middle Ages ever received was in the parish church. In some Oxfordshire churches the medieval wall paintings which once helped to teach religious ideals to a largely illiterate populace have been uncovered and restored. The Doom or Last Judgement was usually painted over the chancel arch and St. Christopher carrying the Christ Child across a river opposite the main entrance. One of the largest and most perfect paintings of this saint is in Horley church. On the chancel walls it was usual to depict a variety of religious stories; those at Chalgrove, dating from about 1350, include 15 scenes from the Life of Christ. The pictures were probably painted by itinerant artists, at least

49

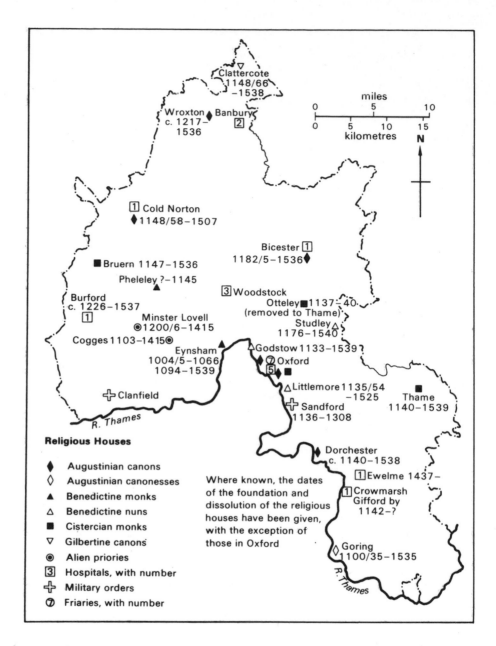

Religious Houses

♦ Augustinian canons
◊ Augustinian canonesses
▲ Benedictine monks
△ Benedictine nuns
■ Cistercian monks
▽ Gilbertine canons
◉ Alien priories
③ Hospitals, with number
✚ Military orders
⑦ Friaries, with number

Where known, the dates of the foundation and dissolution of the religious houses have been given, with the exception of those in Oxford

one of whom—the artist who worked at South Newington in the 14th century—was very skilful.

In spite of all the care lavished on the parish church, it was not always well served. A rector's income came from tithes, glebe land, church offerings, and fees, and in some cases amounted to a sizeable sum. When a rector was unable to serve his church himself or where the church and its income had been given to a monastery or a college a vicar was instituted. The vicar's share of the rector's perquisites was often very small. The bishop of Lincoln considered five marks (£3 6s. 8d.) a suitable basic wage. Nevertheless, the vicar of Albury was paid only 3 marks (£2) in 1254 and there were many like him. Poor stipends had a lowering effect on clerical standards. John de Heyford, Rector of Upper Heyford between 1304 and 1306, was imprisoned as a notorious thief. Many parsons were poorly educated; one vicar of Waterperry was deprived of his living for illiteracy. There was a quick turnover of incumbents; Ambrosden had 25 different vicars in 200 years. They got into debt—in 1317 a vicar was unable to repay a loan of £57. These men may have been the exception rather than the rule, but they were the ones that caught the public attention.

Abbot's Parlour, Thame Abbey

Little interest was shown in the monastic life in Oxfordshire until the 12th century. There may have been religious houses at Oxford and Islip in the 8th century which would have been destroyed during the Danish raids. The Benedictine abbey at Eynsham is the only pre-Conquest religious house in the county for which there is any authentic evidence. It was founded in 1004-5 by Æthelmar. Ælfric, the grammarian and scholar, was its first abbot. It came to an end in 1066 when the monks dispersed, but in 1094-5 Remigius, Bishop of Lincoln, revived it. The abbey was situated on the main road from London to Wales and in the second half of the 12th century complaints were made that it was being impoverished by the duty of offering hospitality to travellers.

In 1122 Gwymund, a royal chaplain, founded St. Frideswide's Priory for Augustinian canons in Oxford. This marked the beginning of the monastic movement in Oxfordshire and other Augustinian houses quickly followed along with those of other orders. Osney Priory for Augustinians was founded in 1129 by Robert d'Oilly, nephew of the Norman sheriff. It was the largest and wealthiest religious house in Oxfordshire and was one of the biggest in England. It was upgraded to the status of abbey in 1154. The abbey acted as bankers for many Oxford people and invested its money in property, building about 1200 the first Golden Cross Inn. Discipline was good and the abbey well run. In 1445 there were 26 canons in residence.

The Cistercians moved into Oxfordshire in 1137 when Robert Gait founded a house at Otteley in Oddington. Three years later it moved to the outskirts of Thame to a site granted by the bishop of Lincoln. Both Thame and Bruern Abbey, founded in 1147 in a remote part of the Cotswolds, participated in sheep farming, though on nothing like the scale of the large Cistercian houses in Yorkshire. In 1224 the abbot of Thame was allowed to carry a load of wool to the Continent in his own ship.

51

*St. Bartholomew's
chapel*

There were four houses for women in the county: Godstow, Studley, Goring, and Littlemore. Of these the most important was Godstow Nunnery near Oxford for Benedictine nuns, founded in 1133 by Dame Edith, widow of William Launceline of Winchester. In a dream she was told to go to Oxford and await a token 'in what wise she should build a place' to God's service. One night a light from heaven shone on the ground and there, at Godstow, she established a nunnery for 24 'of the most gentlewomen that you can find'. The abbey church was dedicated in the presence of the king, queen, archbishop of Canterbury, and many other church dignitaries. Rosamund Clifford, Henry II's mistress, was buried there, and the king favoured the house by helping it financially.

There were also foundations dedicated to the care of the sick and aged. St. Bartholomew's Hospital at Cowley, founded by Henry I for 12 lepers and a chaplain was the first. Its 14th-century chapel is still standing. Others followed at Ewelme, Banbury, and Crowmarsh.

The 13th century saw the advent of the Friars, but whereas the monasteries and nunneries tended to be in the countryside away from the temptations of town life, the Friars made straight for Oxford, attracted by the University. The Dominicans or Blackfriars arrived in 1221 and by 1236 occupied a site south of Littlegate Street. The Franciscans or Greyfriars came in 1224 and settled on a large site south of Church Street. Their church was the largest of any Franciscan house outside London. Many other Orders of Friars followed in the latter part of the 13th and the early part of the 14th centuries. They lived a life of poverty, prayer, preaching, and teaching. They were extremely popular and people flocked to hear them and to join their Orders.

The appeal of the religious life gradually declined. Monks, nuns, and Friars ceased to keep to their ideals of poverty, prayer, and serving the community. Discipline became lax; some houses were seriously in debt; the number of inmates dwindled. Chaucer's view of the monk 'An outridere that lovede venerie (hunting) . . . Ful many a deyntee hors hadde he in stable' and of the Friar 'a wantowne and a merye', was probably applicable to the monks and Friars in Oxfordshire in the late 14th century. Official visitors to the monasteries made increasingly adverse comments about what they saw and tried to enforce codes of discipline without success. At Godstow the visitors heard that 'the scholars of Oxford can have all kinds of good cheer with the nuns to their hearts' content', while the canons of St. Frideswide's Priory wandered about Oxford quite freely. At Littlemore the nuns played and romped with boys in the cloisters and the prioress was rumoured to have an illegitimate daughter. So

52

low had the monasteries sunk in public opinion that Bishop Fox of Winchester's plan that Corpus Christi College, founded in 1516, should be for monks was dropped.

Cold Norton Priory was closed in 1507 when the only inmate died. St. Frideswide's and Littlemore Priories were dissolved in 1524-5 and their incomes given to Cardinal College. Fifteen years later monastic life in Oxfordshire had come to an end. The dismissed abbot of Eynsham received a handsome pension of £133 and was made Bishop of Llandaff; Robert King, Abbot of Osney, became the first Bishop of Oxford; and the abbess of Godstow was given £50 a year. All the property and revenues of the dissolved houses went to the Crown. Some were then redistributed among the Oxford colleges —Eynsham Abbey's estate at Charlbury passed to St. John's College. Or land was leased and sold to men only too eager to increase their holdings. Lord Williams acquired Thame Abbey and the Pope family Wroxton Abbey. Godstow Nunnery was sold for a private house. Many buildings were left to decay or were demolished. Stone from the Carmelite Friary in Oxford was used for buildings at St. John's College and that from the Blackfriars for Trinity College.

Dorchester Abbey church was the only monastic church to survive intact. The church of St. Frideswide's Priory was given a reprieve when half of the nave had already been destroyed. In 1546 what was left became the cathedral church of the new Oxford diocese. The worst of all this destruction was carried out at Osney Abbey. The church was 352 feet long, 100 feet wide, with double aisles and 24 side altars, and it was decided to retain it as the cathedral church. Then there was a change of plan and the buildings were left to decay and were slowly and methodically destroyed. Soon hardly anything remained of what was once a fine and noble building.

Ruins of a chapel, Godstow Abbey

IX Markets and Towns

*Chipping Norton
Gild Hall*

In 1066 Oxford was the only place of any size or importance in the county, and it maintained this position until quite recently. During the Middle Ages, however, several villages began to develop into small market towns, most of them in the northern and western parts of the county.

Banbury, Bicester, and Chipping Norton grew up at road junctions; Witney, Burford, and Henley where an important road crosses a river. Much of Henley's growth in the Middle Ages and later was due to its position on the more easily navigable part of the Thames. Just as good communications helped the development of these places, so the lack of them contributed to the tardy growth of places like Bampton and Watlington.

A market was essential if a village was to develop into a town—it brought trade and money. Bampton had a market in 1086 where agricultural products could be traded, but it was not easily accessible and remained only of local importance. Burford had a market and gild merchant by about 1100 granted by the king to the lord of the manor, and during the 12th and 13th centuries at least 20 weekly markets were opened in Oxfordshire. It was a sure way for a lord to increase his manorial profits; he could collect tolls from those coming to trade and property tended to increase in value. Sometimes the grant of a market was coupled with that of one or more annual fairs. They were even more profitable, bringing traders and buyers from much farther afield and the goods exchanged were more varied.

Some lords went still further to stimulate the growth of towns on their manors as the bishop of Lincoln did at Thame. The original village was a small settlement centred around the church. Then early in the second half of the 12th century the bishop set aside 50 acres of his demesne to form New Thame around what became the High Street. The land was divided into acre and half-acre plots and let to tenants who in return for paying an annual rent were freed from the customary services normally due to the lord. By 1234 there were 63 such tenements. A market, granted by the king in about 1184, was held each week in the widest part of the High Street, and in 1219 the bishop obtained the king's permission to divert the main road away from its existing route by the church to pass down the High Street and through the market. The Cistercian Abbey on the

54

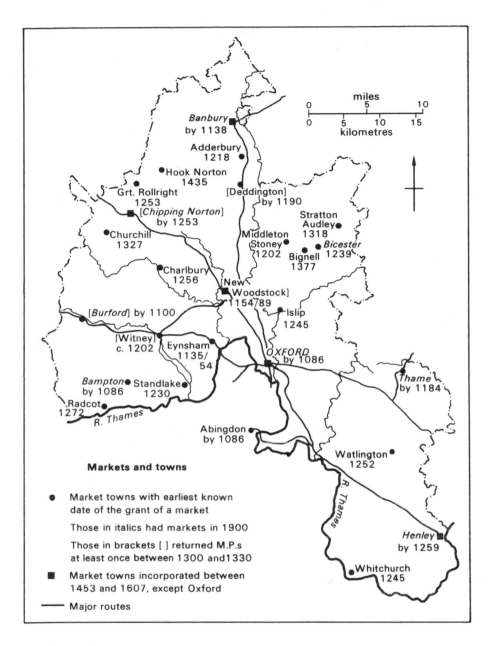

miles
0   5   10

0   5   10   15
kilometres

Banbury
by 1138

Adderbury
1218

●Hook Norton
1435

Grt. Rollright
1253

[Deddington]
by 1190

[*Chipping Norton*]
by 1253

Stratton
Audley●
1318

●Churchill
1327

Middleton
Stoney●
?1202

Bicester 1239●

Bignell
1377

●Charlbury
1256

[New
Woodstock]
1154/89

●Islip
1245

[*Burford*] by 1100

[Witney]
c. 1202

Eynsham
1135/
54

OXFORD
by 1086

Bampton●
by 1086

Standlake●
1230

Thame
by 1184

●Radcot
1272

R. Thames

Abingdon
by 1086

Watlington
1252

R. Thames

Henley
by 1259

Whitchurch
1245

Markets and towns

●   Market towns with earliest known
date of the grant of a market

Those in italics had markets in 1900

Those in brackets [ ] returned M.P.s
at least once between 1300 and 1330

■   Market towns incorporated between
1453 and 1607, except Oxford

—— Major routes

outskirts of Thame and the prebendal household at Priest End brought additional trade and travellers to the town. Similarly, religious houses helped to foster the growth of Bicester and Eynsham.

Banbury also belonged to the bishop of Lincoln and here, too, expansion was deliberately encouraged in the late 12th century. In the 13th century the bishop allowed Newland to be laid out in plots for tenements. By the early 13th century there were about 1,300

55

Butter Cross, Witney

people in Banbury and in 1441 about 1,600, making it the second largest town in the county.

Although the abbot of Eynsham was granted a weekly market at Charlbury in 1256 it was given little encouragement, and in 1440 it was 'inconvenient and useless'. At Eynsham itself, however, the abbot set aside about 20 acres in 1215 as building plots for letting to tenants at 4*s.* an acre a year, and by 1336 there were 31 houses on the land.

Of all the lords in the county, the king was the most important, and it was Henry II who founded the royal borough of New Woodstock. The reason for his actions was recorded later in 1279 in the Hundred Rolls. 'There was a certain empty plot beside the park of the manor of Woodstock and since the king's men were lodged too far from the manor, the king gave divers parcels of land from the said empty plot to men who would come and build hospicia . . .'. By that time there were 137 houses and a population of about 540. Old Woodstock which lay either side of the Oxford to Banbury road remained quite separate from this new settlement.

Some of the places to which markets were granted never prospered. Radcot, Standlake, Stratton Audley, and Middleton Stoney were granted markets and fairs but they can only have survived for a short time. Radcot was too near to Bampton and Faringdon, and Stratton Audley and Middleton Stoney too close to Bicester. Others did prosper, like Thame, where there were men of local importance and wealth based on trade. Robert Elys was a wool merchant of some standing in the 14th century and Geoffrey Dormer, whose monument is in the church, was a merchant of the Calais Staple in the 15th century. Richard Quatremaine was employed in the London customs. At Bicester the Black Death struck the town severely and profits from the market fell sharply. However, in 1622 it had a 'very good market for all manner of cattle and well supplied with all kinds of trade'.

Banbury, Witney, Chipping Norton, and Burford all benefited from the Cotswold wool trade. When Leland visited Banbury between 1535 and 1543 he remarked on the very 'celebrate market there'. The town had aquired fame for its cloth and ale in the 13th, and for its cheeses in the 15th, and subsequent centuries. What prosperity could do for a town can still be seen at Burford. Stone houses replaced earlier wooden ones, tenements were divided and re-divided, and the back gardens built up, and finally new houses were built up the hill away from the old town centre near the river and church, and in 1547 there were about 825 people living in Burford.

All the market towns were administered by manorial officials. A Portmoot was held by the bailiff or reeve where cases of debt,

56

trespass, breaches of the peace, and selling bad food were heard. In a few places a form of self-government was gradually acquired. Henley had a gild merchant which regulated trade, maintained the bridge over the Thames, and tried to keep the town clean and wholesome. At Burford the gild merchant assumed many of the powers which really belonged to the lord of the manor and which they had no right to exercise. The lord lived far away and his officials were lazy. By 1250 some of the gild members had formed themselves into an executive body and had their own seal. In 1500 the executive consisted of an alderman and 14 burgesses and they were running the market, collecting tolls, making bye-laws, and holding a court which in 1561 met in the Tolsey. In 1617-19 their right to do these things was challenged by Sir Lawrence Tanfield, the new lord of the manor, and they were found guilty of usurping his privileges—in future they were to manage only the charity lands. Burford reverted to full manorial control.

Burford Seal

After Oxford, the next town to receive a charter of incorporation was New Woodstock in 1453. In 1526 Henry VIII granted the warden and others of the gild merchant of Henley certain liberties and privileges including control of fairs, the assay of wine and victuals, and the right to choose a coroner. In 1568 a second charter set the government in the hands of a warden, two portreeves, and 12 capital burgesses. Banbury was incorporated in 1554 in recognition of its loyalty to Queen Mary. Chipping Norton was the last town in the county to receive a charter—in 1607—which gave control to two bailiffs and 12 burgesses whose first step was to introduce stringent trade regulations.

Even the largest of these towns was small, consisting for the most part of only a few streets. The centre of the town lay around the market place, and these large open spaces are still a feature of many of them, as at Deddington, Thame, which still has a weekly market, Chipping Norton, and Henley. There were no amenities or luxuries. Life revolved around the church, the market, and the open fields where many of a town's inhabitants held and farmed land. The most important secular buildings were the market or gild halls, some of which still exist as at Witney, Chipping Norton, and Burford. Interests were local and when the demand came early in the 14th century to send representatives to Parliament it was received without enthusiasm and avoided if possible. It was not until the late 16th century that this attitude was reversed and townsmen began to look beyond their own locality.

X   A Little Learning

John Stanbridge

The earliest schools in Oxfordshire were either part of a religious gild or chantry, or of one of the colleges in Oxford. Latin grammar was the subject most commonly and thoroughly taught, for a sound knowledge of it was essential for entrance to University, to the Church, and to the legal and medical professions. In Oxford masters opened grammar schools attached to Merton College in about 1270 and to New College and Queen's College in the 14th century. Here founders' kin and poor boys could receive the Latin tuition necessary for them to continue their studies in the University. Then William of Waynflete, Bishop of Winchester, founded Magdalen College School in 1479, which still flourishes today. Here any boy could be educated free of charge. The master was paid £10 a year and the usher £5 together with free board and lodging. It opened in the crypt of the chapel of the Hospital of St. John the Baptist and a very high standard of teaching was achieved, for the masters were scholarly men of excellent reputation. During the late 15th and 16th centuries the school was considered to be far superior to Winchester College.

Outside Oxford, until the 16th century, there were few opportunities for boys to be taught unless their parents could pay for private tutoring. In 1501 John Stanbridge was chosen by St. John's Hospital, Banbury, to be their schoolmaster. It was an admirable choice for Stanbridge was a man of considerable ability, 'a right worthy lover of his faculty and an indefatigable man in teaching and writing'. He had been educated at Winchester and New College and had been Master of Magdalen College School. He pioneered changes in the way Latin grammar was taught and wrote what was probably the first Latin grammar in the English tongue. He made the school famous and his teaching methods were widely copied. The statutes of the Manchester Free Grammar School drawn up in 1515 and 1525 declared that the High Master was to 'teach children grammar after the school use, manner and form of the school of Banbury . . . which is called Stanbridge grammar'.

The other schools in the county at this time were at Ewelme, Henley, Witney, Chipping Norton, and Deddington. At Burford members of the Gild of Our Lady had built a chapel on to the parish church where a priest said masses and taught children free of charge.

Local people seemed well-pleased with the education their children received in these gild and chantry schools. In 1546 the masters at Burford and Chipping Norton were 'well-learned', and at Deddington the master 'bringeth up youth very well in learning'.

The chantries and gilds were abolished during the Reformation and with them most of the schools. It was an unpopular decision, and in Oxford the uproar was so great that Magdalen College School was allowed to continue, as were the schools at Ewelme and Chipping Norton.

*Nixon's School,
Oxford*

The gap left by the closures was eventually filled by endowed grammar schools which provided a free classical education for boys. Some were founded by clergyman like Christopher Rawlins, Vicar of Adderbury and a Fellow of New College. He endowed a school at Adderbury in 1589 for up to 50 boys. He requested that the local inhabitants should help with 'their carts and carriages to carry some clay, lime or timber, or any other necessary thing for the building thereof'.

The schools at Williamscot (1574) and Woodstock (1585) were founded by merchants and that at Thame (1559) by the statesman, Lord Williams. At Burford the bailiffs and townsmen took the initiative, moved it was said 'by the great number of youth and children that may be from time to time in the said town . . ., their parents unable to keep them at school, by which means they have spent their time idly and had not been traded and brought up in good order of learning or knowledge whereby they might know their duty to God, their Prince, and their parents and obtain increase in vitrue and learning . . .'. What better reasons could there be than these for founding a school?

By the close of the 16th century, four new schools had been opened in Oxfordshire and three of the suppressed ones re-endowed. In the next century Henley and Witney schools were refounded and six new ones established. One of these was in Oxford where Alderman John Nixon offered to pay £30 a year to a master if the city Council provided a schoolroom. It opened in 1658 in the Council chamber, and a year later a proper school was built in the court of the Town Hall. It was intended for 40 boys who were to be the sons of poor freemen or the kin of the founder and Town Clerk. Boys were to be taken on payment of an entrance fee of 12d. at nine or ten years of age and they could stay for up to seven years. They were to be taught reading, writing, and arithmetic and Latin, which together were considered more suitable for boys of their background than a purely classical education.

The children who attend Ewelme Primary School are still taught in the 15th-century grammar school building. At Thame also the

59

Lord Williams's Grammar School, Thame

Tudor grammar school, though no longer used as a school, has been preserved. On the ground floor were the classroom, only 50 feet by 20 feet, and two small rooms for the private use of the master and usher. Upstairs each had a bedroom and the master was allowed the use of a library attached to the porch and of the attic to accommodate boarders, but there were no rooms for a master's wife and family.

A typical day at a grammar school began with prayers or church, for great care was taken to give the boys a good grounding in the principles of the Protestant religion. This was followed by the master hearing grammar recited by heart and seeing that it was understood. The master read lessons daily and the boys repeated them back. Nine or ten hours in summer and six in winter were spent this way. It must have been dull and tedious for even the most diligent scholar, and games, if allowed at all, were very restricted. Harsh treatment by the masters was not uncommon to judge from a regulation made at Dorchester grammar school that boys were not to be beaten on the head or have their ears, nose and cheek pinched or hair pulled.

Private schools providing a classical education were opened from time to time. In 1669 Samuel Blackwell, Vicar of Bicester, taught boys in a side chapel of the parish church and they lodged with the vicar and his wife. The standard of teaching was considered to be so good by the local gentry that they preferred to send their sons to Mr. Blackwell rather than to Eton or Winchester. When he became ill the school declined and closed.

By the early 18th century the grammar schools were well past their prime. School incomes were insufficient to pay for repairs to buildings; the study of Latin and Greek was giving way to instruction in reading, writing, and arithmetic, for great difficulties were experienced in getting suitably qualified masters. In 1758 there were only five boys at the Henley school, and eight years later the master was dismissed for being absent for days at a time. The master appointed to the Dorchester School in 1746 was not qualified to teach Latin grammar. In 1808 the salary of £17 10s. together with the master's house and fees from paying scholars offered to the master of Steeple Aston school were insufficient to attract candidates when a vacancy arose. By 1818 the Banbury school buildings were being let to a manufacturer of plush and the school at Burford was 'totally decayed'. Only Thame, Witney, and Henley grammar schools survived into the 20th century, and these have now been absorbed into schemes for comprehensive education.

Just as the chantry and gild schools had been replaced by the grammar schools, now they in turn gave way to the elementary or

60

charity schools for the education of poor children. They were founded and endowed by a host of well-meaning men and women for both boys and girls. Although the first charity school in Oxfordshire opened at Somerton in 1580, they did not become common until the 18th century when 20 were set up. Typical of these was the Blue Coat School at Banbury, founded in 1705 by voluntary subscription. The school was held in rooms over the town gaol and here the master, paid £25 a year and able to understand arithmetic and write a good hand, taught 30 boys writing and arithmetic. A mistress taught 20 girls to knit, sew, and spin, and a selected few also learnt to write. Both boys and girls were given blue outfits to wear, from which the school took its name. Great emphasis was laid on teaching the principles of the Christian faith, and on leaving school many of the children received a Bible or prayer book.

18th-century schoolgirl

The Nonconformists also took a keen interest in education. There was a Quaker schoolmaster at Charlbury in 1663 and at Banbury in 1708. In 1717 the Witney Quakers promised their schoolmaster six boarders and 12 weekly scholars and 'young women that may be willing to improve their learning'.

Nevertheless, there was still a deplorable shortage of educational facilities in the county and this emerged only too clearly in 1738. The clergy were asked for details about schools in their respective parishes and most had to admit there were none. In some the clergy tried to fill the gap as at Finmere where the incumbent paid for the children to be taught to read. In others the lord of the manor made some provision—at Buckwell he paid for most of the poor children to learn to read and say the Catechism. In Oxford there was virtually no schooling for those who could not pay. In 1708 the Grey Coat School was founded, where 54 boys, mainly the sons of college servants, were taught reading, writing, accounts, and the principles of religion; they were paid for by the colleges.

The 19th century saw a great expansion in education, mainly through the activity of religious bodies. Sunday Schools were opened in great numbers and were very important in providing the only education there was for large groups of children. For many, Sunday was the one day in the week that they were not working. The instruction given sometimes included reading lessons, but mostly it was learning by heart from the Bible and prayer book. To improve this situation, the Nonconformist British and Foreign Bible Society and the Church of England Anglican National Society began setting up day schools. A British school was opened in Charlbury in 1815 and a National school for boys and girls in 1817 at Banbury. Others quickly followed. When the clergy were asked for information about

61

Garsington school in the early 19th century

schools in 1854 it was clear from their answers that great strides had been made. In Oxford, for example, all but one parish now had a school or schools. Even so the heartfelt comment of the incumbent at Blackbourton shows how much more needed to be done: 'My great want is a day school. I am shorn of my strength entirely for want of one. I could use the school for evening lectures and otherwise instructing my poor ignorant congregation'. At Cottisford land was available but the incumbent could see no way of raising the money to pay for the buildings.

Dame schools sprang up in great numbers—there were seven in Adderbury alone in 1831. Very little was taught at these schools, for the mistresses or masters (for some dames were men) were often as ignorant as their pupils. Private schools and academies abounded, especially in Oxford. At Bloxham in 1853, the Rev. J. W. Hewett founded a Church of England boarding school for the sons of the professional classes. In 1896 it was handed over to the Society of Woodard Schools. In Banbury Sir Bernhard Samuelson financed the Cherwell British school which opened in 1861, and in 1884 he gave a new building for the rapidly expanding Mechanics' Institute for adult education.

There was, of course, opposition to these expanding educational facilities. People at Adderbury considered any education, however little, would spoil girls for domestic service. Many of the clergy did not consider writing and arithmetic suitable subjects for poor children to be taught for fear of educating them beyond their station in life. Many parents could not afford to have their children at school. At Mixbury in 1854 the children were leaving school at eight or nine years of age to work in the fields or make lace. The boys left Yarnton school as soon as they could, and at Pyrton they stayed away to help feed the cattle.

Towards the latter part of the 19th century Parliament began to intervene in educational affairs, and in 1870 the first Elementary Education Act was passed, providing for the setting up of School Boards in areas where there were more children than school places. Banbury managed to reorganise its schools so that a board was not necessary, but one had to be established at Oxford. From this time onwards it was recognised that all children should receive some form of elementary education and the existing charity and church schools were gradually incorporated into a state system. Secondary education for all had to wait until the 20th century.

62

XI   The Civil War

Trouble had been brewing for the Stuart kings long before hostilities began in 1642. Rebellions in Scotland and Ireland, unsuccessful campaigns in France and Spain, unpopular changes in church ritual, and dubiously legal taxation all made for increasingly bad feeling between king and people. In Oxfordshire, William Fiennes, Viscount Saye and Sele of Broughton, was a vocal opponent of the king and his policies and in 1622 he was imprisoned in the Fleet for speaking against James I. His home at Broughton Castle was a secret meeting-place for men with similar ideas. According to Anthony Wood, the antiquary, there was 'a room and passage thereunto, which his servants were prohibited to come near; and when they were of a complete number, there would be great noise and talkings heard among them, . . . yet could they never discern their lord's companions'. These unknown companions were in fact John Hampden, John Pym, Sir Henry Vane, and the Earl of Essex—all critics of the king. Fiennes became known as 'Old Subtilty' for his cunning and caution. One 17th-century historian described him as 'a seriously subtil peece, and always averse to the Court wayes, something out of pertinaciousnesse' with a preference for going 'contrary to the wind'. But he disapproved strongly of the execution of Charles I in 1649 and lived quietly thereafter at Broughton until his death in 1662. He may have encouraged the people of Banbury in their refusal to pay their full quota of the very unpopular ship money levy. Mayors there tried in vain to collect the tax.

Sir William Compton

When actual war broke out in 1642, towns, villages, and even families were left divided in their loyalties. In north Oxfordshire Viscount Saye and Sele was of course for Parliament and he raised a regiment and garrisoned his house which at one time was besieged by the Royalists. He and his sons fought for Parliament at the battle of Edgehill. To some extent his influence was counter-balanced by the Royalist Earl of Northampton, whose home, Compton Wynyates, was just in Warwickshire. The earl's third son, William Compton, was knighted in 1643 for his gallant leadership in an attack on Banbury when two horses were shot from under him. He, and two others of his family, were governors of the royalist garrison at Banbury. Henry Danvers of Cornbury Park sent the king £3,400 for his cause and tried to ensure that when he died his estate did not pass to his

63

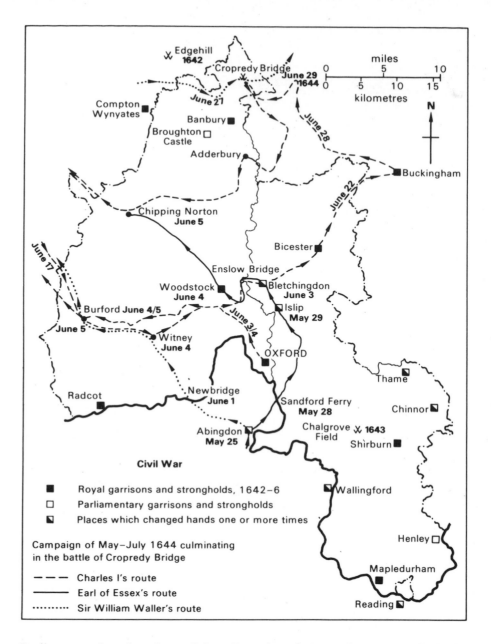

miles
0   5   10
0   5   10   15
kilometres

N

Civil War

■   Royal garrisons and strongholds, 1642–6
□   Parliamentary garrisons and strongholds
◨   Places which changed hands one or more times

Campaign of May–July 1644 culminating
in the battle of Cropredy Bridge

– – –   Charles I's route
———   Earl of Essex's route
··········   Sir William Waller's route

Parliamentarian brother. John French of Broughton supplied the
Royalists with malt while his son was physician to a Parliamentarian
force.

In the south of the county there were the staunch Royalist and
Catholic families of Tanner, Blount, and Stonor. Mapledurham House,
the home of Sir Charles Blount, was besieged and plundered by
Cromwell's troops. At Shirburn, Sir John Chamberlain insisted that

20.   The first Cuddesdon Palace was built by Bishop Bancroft in 1634-5 for the use of the bishops of Oxford. Destroyed during the Civil War in 1644 as a precaution against Parliamentary occupation, it was restored in 1679 by Bishop Fell.

21.   This contemporary plan of the defences of Oxford was the work of Sir Bernard de Gomme, a Dutch military engineer, who served Charles I.

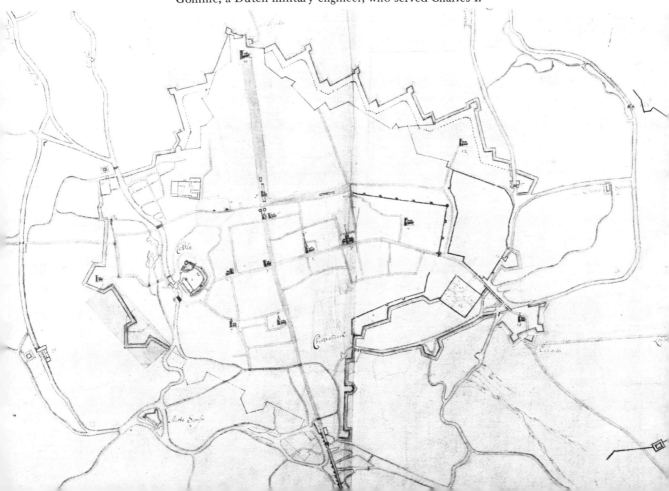

22.   Tom Tower, Christ Church, the work of Thomas Wolsey and Christopher Wre

his tenants' leases contained a provision that they would fight for the king if it was necessary. The common soldier pressed into an army to fight for a cause he probably did not understand often chose the side that paid the best, 'they care not for whom they fight so they have but money', and changing sides was not uncommon.

The war became a reality in Oxfordshire after the battle of Edgehill in October 1642, when Charles I made Oxford his headquarters. Here, as might be expected, Town and Gown were ranged on opposite sides. As far as was possible the townsmen followed a policy of non-co-operation with the Royalist garrison. It was only with great reluctance that they helped with the construction of fortifications. The students showed great eagerness to help, and as an eyewitness reported, 'do night and day gall their hands with mattocks and shovels'. Although the town was naturally defended on three sides by rivers, these were added to by earthworks 'very high, having many strong bulwarks so regularly flanking one another, that nothing could be more exactly done'. The river Cherwell was made to flood and booms were placed across the Thames.

The John Hampden Memorial, Chalgrove

The townsmen were reluctant to raise a regiment for their own defence and complained, when asked to pay £200 a week towards the cost of the fortifications, that they were already contributing £120 to the city regiment. But many citizens grew rich at the army's expense, profiting from the increased demand for food, drink, and beds. On the debit side there were outbreaks of camp fever in 1643 and plague in 1644 because of overcrowding and insanitary conditions, and there was much brawling and unruly behaviour. Some leading citizens like Alderman John Nixon preferred to leave the town and were disfranchised by the king's order.

The king and his court resided at Christ Church and the queen at Merton. The Royal Mint moved into New Inn Hall Street. Gunpowder was made at Osney Mill, ammunition was kept at New College, and cloth, oats, ropes, and other provisions were stored in the Schools. The king asked for and was allowed the first crop of hay off Port-meadow. Town and Gown alike were asked to give up their brass and other metal ware to be made into weapons, and the colleges relinquished their plate to be minted into coins.

Studies at the University were seriously disrupted. Students caught up in the excitement of war were 'much debauched and became idle by their bearing arms and keeping company with rude soldiers'. William Beau of Merton equipped with arms several of his own students, and Peter Turner, Savilian Professor of Geometry, who was over 50 years old, joined the army. With so many University and college buildings commandeered for the use of the king and his army, there was a

65

Cropredy Bridge and inscription

shortage of accommodation for students and lectures had to be given in St. Mary the Virgin church.

It was from Oxford that Prince Rupert marched in 1643 to rout a Parliamentary force at the battle of Chalgrove Field. During the fight John Hampden was mortally wounded and died a few days later at Thame. In 1644 Sir William Waller and the Earl of Essex tried to encircle Oxford and seize the king. Charles managed to escape at night, marching out of the town with several thousand troops, passing between his two enemies without being detected. Waller pursued him as far as Burford and then joined Essex at Chipping Norton. From there Essex went to the relief of Lyme, while Waller followed Charles into Warwickshire. On his return to Oxfordshire the king forced Waller to fight at Cropredy Bridge. Although it was a Royalist victory any good it did their cause was reversed a few weeks later when Prince Rupert was defeated at Marston Moor. The king continued to use Oxford as his base until April 1646 when he left to go to northern England. He never returned and in June that year the city surrendered to the Parliamentarians. The fortifications were demolished and life gradually returned to normal.

For four years Oxfordshire had been disturbed and disrupted by skirmishes, raids, pillaging, burning, and looting. Both sides levied taxes and commandeered provisions, for the armies lived off the land. In 1642 the king ordered the parishes around Oxford to bring him straw, hay, oats and corn, and complaints that nothing had been paid for were ignored. The inhabitants of Ploughley hundred were made to bring their carts for the conveyance of ammunition, and when 2,000 horses were taken out of the county for military use in 1643, people had to pool their resources to make up teams for ploughing. At Thame the grammar school was used as a garrison and hospital, and the market was held only with difficulty. In 1643 the Royalists seized all the fat cattle bought by the London butchers at Thame market. Chinnor was set on fire by the Royalists to prevent its re-occupation by the enemy, and when a tax became due, people who could not pay were forced to give up their clothes and linen. The bishop of Oxford's palace at Cuddesdon, completed only in 1634, was scorched by a Royalist as a precaution against its being occupied by the enemy, and at Godstow the former nunnery, now a private house, was destroyed in 1645 lest it fall into Parliamentarian hands.

Wood and timber were destroyed in large quantities. At one time over 400 men were cutting down trees on Shotover, while on another occasion men were told to come with axes, hatchets, and bills for lopping trees and cutting up hedges in St. Clement's parish and on

66

Headington Hill, 'for the better discovery of the enemy and the freer passage for shooting'. White clay was dug on Shotover for tobacco pipes for soldiers stationed in Oxford and salt petre was dug near Kings Sutton in Northamptonshire to supply gunpowder made near Banbury.

Banbury suffered quite severe damage during the Civil War. The castle was in Parliamentary hands until the king forced it to surrender after the battle of Edgehill. It was besieged by the Parliamentarians from July to October 1644, when 30 houses near the castle were burnt and others pulled down. After the second siege in 1646 the town had 'scarce the one half standing to gaze on the ruins of the other'. It was certainly an exaggeration, but Parliament granted £300 worth of timber sequestered from a Royalist and timber and stone from the demolished castle, towards reconstruction.

With the surrender of Oxford in June 1646, and Banbury a month earlier, the war came to an end for Oxfordshire. Little happened in connection with national affairs during the remainder of the war or under the Commonwealth. In 1649, however, the Levellers—extremist democrats in Cromwell's army—caused disturbances at Banbury, Oxford, and Burford, where three of the rebels were shot *pour encourager les autres*. The Restoration of the Monarchy and the return of Charles II were warmly welcomed in the county, for opinions had changed. In Oxford where Parliament's cause had once found favour, bells were rung and bonfires lit to celebrate the occasion.

XII   Reformation and Nonconformity

Burford church

John Wycliffe, Fellow of Merton and Master of Balliol, had begun to question the authority of the Pope and priesthood in general by 1374. Between that date and his death in 1384 he went on to deny the doctrine of transubstantiation and to criticise abuses in the Church. His ideas were not new and they aroused a limited amount of interest in the University, but his criticisms of the Church met with some approval among ordinary folk at a time when anti-clerical feelings were already running high. His followers became known as Lollards and the scholars among them translated the Bible into English for the first time. Lollardy lingered on in parts of Oxfordshire for many years. James Wyllys, a weaver and a 'lettred' man, who came originally from Bristol where he had learnt his heresy, was arrested at Henley in 1462 and was excommunicated and burnt to death. There were heretics at Thame and Chinnor in 1464. In 1522 a conventicle was meeting in secret at Burford, while other Lollards were known to be living at Asthall, Witney, Standlake, and Henley. One of the Burford Lollards had paid the large sum of £1 for an English Bible. These heretics, many of them weavers, were rounded up and made to do penance. On market day they stood on the step of Burford Cross for 15 minutes with faggots on their shoulders, and on Sunday they led a procession in church, bearing the faggots, and knelt throughout the service on the altar steps. Finally, so that all might know of their erring ways, they were branded on the cheek.

The Lollards were not alone in criticising the Church and there was much that needed reforming. During the bishop's visitation of 1517 many churches were found to be in a bad state of repair—at Brightwell Baldwin, for example, the chancel was ruinous and there was no glass in the windows. In 1526 nearly two-thirds of the incumbents were non-resident and church services were neglected or not said in a proper manner. The religious houses were increasingly unpopular and their dissolution was welcomed. But people petitioned against the suppression of chantries, and the endowments, which in many cases amounted to very little, were allowed to be used for the poor. Some plate and jewels were taken by the Crown, but it was unscrupulous churchwardens that were responsible for the loss of many church treasures at this time. In 1552 the inhabitants of Thame complained that silver chalices, crosses, and bowls had been

68

sold for over £300, and that the churchwardens had pocketed the proceeds.

The severance of connections between the Church in England and the Papacy in Rome in 1533-4 was accomplished with little opposition from the clergy in Oxfordshire. But Sir Adrian Fortescue of Stonor Park, a man of local importance, spoke out vehemently against the king's policies, refused to take the Oath of Supremacy, and joined a conspiracy to return England to papal control. His reward was imprisonment and then, in 1539, he was beheaded.

Ten years later the government's insistence that the first English Prayer Book must be used in all churches led to a brief uprising among outraged yeoman and clergy in Oxfordshire and Buckinghamshire. The leader of the Oxfordshire contingent was probably James Webbe, Vicar of Barford St. Michael. They were easily quashed as Edward VI noted: 'To Oxon. the lord Grey of Wilton was sent with 1500 horsemen and footmen; whose coming with th'assembling of the gentlemen of the countrie, did so abash the rebels, that more than hauf of them rann ther wayes, and other that tarried were some slain, some taken, and some hanged'. Among those who died for their stand against the new doctrine was the vicar of Chipping Norton, condemned to hang upon the steeple of his church.

In 1542 Henry VIII established six new episcopal sees, Oxford being one of them. The boundaries of the new diocese were almost the same as those of the county. In 1836 Berkshire, and in 1845 Buckinghamshire, were added. The first Bishop of Oxford was Robert King, former Abbot of Thame and Osney Abbeys. He seems to have been a tolerant man and was able to keep his position under both Edward VI and Mary. Mary being a devout Catholic, the changes in doctrine and ritual introduced by her father and brother were reversed during her reign. In Banbury this was greeted with some hostility but a Protestant martyr was burned there. In 1555-6 Hugh Latimer, Bishop of Worcester, Nicholas Ridley, Bishop of London, and Thomas Cranmer, Archbishop of Canterbury, were all burned at the stake in Broad Street, Oxford, outside the doors of Balliol College. Their imprisonment in the Bocardo gaol and their deaths seem to have passed without local comment—perhaps through indifference, or more likely from fear.

With Elizabeth's accession reform returned. The churchwardens at South Newington who had purchased vestments and a cope during Mary's reign now bought a Prayer Book, Bible, and Book of Homilies in English. Attitudes began to harden during the remainder of the 16th century and the division between reformers and those who adhered to the old ways widened. In the north of the county the

Christ Church Cathedral, spire and tower

69

Sir Anthony Cope

Copes of Hanwell, and to a lesser extent, the Fiennes of Broughton, wanted church reform taken much further than Queen Elizabeth would allow. Sir Anthony Cope composed a new prayer book and took the bold step of moving in the House of Commons in 1587-8 that it should form the basis of future doctrine. Elizabeth, wanting at all costs to keep Parliament from meddling in church affairs, had him imprisoned for the rest of that session. In Banbury where the two families had some influence, people were increasingly Puritan in outlook and 'A Banbury Man' became another name for a Puritan. In the south of the county the Stonor family adhered to the old faith and their home at Stonor Park became the rallying point for local Roman Catholics. In 1580 a Jesuit Mission was launched from there and leading Jesuits like Father Campion were visitors. In the 17th century and later many members of the Stonor family were heavily fined or imprisoned for refusing to give up their faith.

Among the earliest organised groups of dissenters to appear in Oxfordshire were the Quakers. In 1654 Elizabeth Heavens and Elizabeth Fletcher 'came under a religious concern to exhort the inhabitants . . ., and the scholars (of Oxford) . . . to repentance and amendment of life'. Their mission was greeted with derision and hostility, especially among the students who 'drove them by force to the pump in John's College, where they pumped water upon their necks, and into their mouths, till they were almost dead'. Despite the mayor's protest, they were sentenced by the Vice-Chancellor of the University to be whipped out of the city. There were many like the cleric of Warborough who 'when in his cups, would go with his comrades to the Quaker meetings to make sport of them'. Even in and around Banbury where local influential men like Bray Doyley, lord of the manor of Adderbury, joined the movement, there were unpleasant scenes. In 1661 soldiers burst in on a Quaker meeting at Banbury and 'barbarously abused the Assembly, beating and bruising many of them'. William Fiennes, Lord Saye and Sele, wrote acrimonious pamphlets about them. Even so, by the early 18th century the Banbury Meeting held a prominent place in the Quaker organisation.

In 1662 some 26 clergy were ejected from their livings in Oxfordshire by the restored Charles II and his ministers for their Puritan or Presbyterian leanings. One of them, Samuel Wells, ejected from Banbury, became minister to a group of people who chose to leave the parish church to form the Presbyterian 'Old Meeting'. Congregational churches opened in Witney and Henley about 1662 and there were several Baptist Meetings in the county by the close of the 17th century.

70

The Nonconformist chapels and churches were supported by people from all walks of life, but they appealed especially to labourers, the poor, and the illiterate, for whom there was little comfort or understanding in the parish church. The same ills which had dogged the Church at the time of the Reformation still existed. In 1738 the vicar of Beckley lived in Oxford where he was chaplain of New College. His income was too small to pay a resident curate. In 1745 the vicarage was 'almost ready to drop down'. The clergy were very critical of their parishioners. The vicar of Bampton reported in 1738 that those of the 'lowest rank' absented themselves from the church 'with a view to Profit or Pleasure or Both; others out of laziness making it a Day of Rest in the worst sense'.

Burford Methodist chapel

About this time John and Charles Wesley were meeting with others in Oxford to read the Bible and pray together in an endeavour to find a more disciplined religious life. They visited the sick and the prisoners in the Castle prison, and opened a Sunday School for poor children. Both the Wesleys were ordained ministers in the Church of England and John Wesley encouraged their followers to attend their parish churches. However, their views and ideals met with considerable opposition both from the University and from other clergy who closed their churches to them. In this way the Methodists, as their followers became known, had no choice but to open their own chapels. Oxford remained hostile to John Wesley, and when he returned in 1751 to preach there he wrote of his surprise to find 'There was no pointing, no calling of names, as once; no, nor even laughter'. In the county he had a mixed reception. As time went by his reputation grew and Methodism spread rapidly especially among the poor. In 1739 he preached at Burford to over 1,200 people, and in 1764 at Witney to large and attentive congregations. 'This is such a people as I have not seen', he wrote in his Journal, 'so remarkably diligent in business and at the same time of so quiet a spirit, and so calm and civil in their behaviour'. From Witney he went to Henley where he 'found a wild staring congregation, many of them void both of commonsense and common decency. I spoke exceeding plain to them all, and reproved them sharply'. When he returned there in 1768 'one or two of the baser sort made some noise, but I reproved them, and, for once, they were ashamed'.

The 19th century saw a revival in the Anglican Church. In Oxford Newman, Froude, Keble, and Pusey initiated the Oxford Movement which stressed the catholicity of the Church of England and its continuity with the early and medieval Church. Its authors wanted to enrich the spiritual life of the Church by an increase in the number of services, particularly Communions, and later by beautifying both

Martyrs' Memorial, Oxford

buildings and services. They saw the need for new churches and Newman was responsible for the erection of a church at Littlemore in 1836. The Movement was regarded with suspicion by many, especially after Newman became a Roman Catholic. The Martyrs' Memorial was put up in Oxford in 1841 to remind people of the achievements of the Reformation and to counteract the Movement's feared Romanising influence. Samuel Wilberforce, Bishop of Oxford from 1845 until 1869, did much to foster the rejuvenation of church activities. The Visitation returns of 1854 show how much had been achieved. Non-residency and absenteeism among the clergy had decreased. Some of the clergy were men of great ability and energy, like William Wilson, Vicar of Banbury in 1849, who brought about a great revival in church work in a place noted for its nonconformity. Dissent was still a problem; the vicar of Chipping Norton estimated that two-fifths of the population of the town attended nonconformist services. The incumbent at Alvescote admitted that 'the doctrine of the dissenting preacher is more palatable and the style more intelligible to the poor than that of the Church of England minister'. By the end of the century many churches had been restored or rebuilt by enthusiastic Victorians. The number of church services was greatly increased and educational and social activities extended. But the religious zeal both of the Anglicans and the Nonconformists was not enough to stop the decline in church membership and the closure of chapels and churches has become an all-too-common feature in Oxfordshire and elsewhere.

XIII Enclosure and After

Enclosure of the open fields on a large scale did not become general in Oxfordshire until after 1758. Between that date and 1882 when the last Inclosure Act was passed, thousands and thousands of acres of arable and waste land had been enclosed.

It was by no means a new idea. In 1517 an Inquiry into enclosure and its effects reported that 8,570 acres of arable had been enclosed in Oxfordshire, three-quarters of which had been converted to pasture, and that 626 people had been evicted or thrown out of work between 1489 and 1517 because there was no land for them to farm. There was little else for the evicted to do, and those dismissed from Binsey manor 'led an evil and wretched existence until life ended', and those dispossessed by the abbot of Eynsham from Little Rollright left 'in tears'.

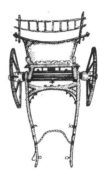

Woodstock waggon

In the 16th century farming became very profitable. When the religious houses were dissolved their vast estates became available for redistribution. In Bletchingdon alone Godstow Nunnery had owned 214 acres and Osney Abbey 77 acres. The Oxford colleges acquired many of the monastic holdings and the rest was quickly bought up or leased by eager laymen. Many of these new landowners were seldom resident on their estates, and during the 16th and early 17th centuries the yeoman farmer came to the fore. He benefited from inflated prices while his labour costs remained steady. His profits were spent on acquiring more land and better stock. In Little Milton, as in many other farm villages all over the Midlands and southern England, the yeomen improved their homes. Their cramped wooden houses, often with only one up and one down, were replaced by larger stone houses with six or more rooms. Staircases replaced ladders, and fireplaces and windows were reconstructed.

For others, however, it was a wretched time. At Bletchingdon the lord of the manor, Vincent Poure, turned out tenants when their leases expired and re-let their holdings at exorbitant rents. He and members of his family enclosed so much land that some people on the manor were left with only three acres to cultivate. In 1596 Francis Poure enclosed 96 acres and there was talk of 'decayed cottagers'. The dispossessed here and at Hampton Gay and other villages in the area could stand no more, and about 300 men met together to sack Poure's house and to 'throw his hedges and those that

73

Oxford Down ram

made them into the ditches'. All was to no avail, however, for in 1622 the lord of the manor, rector, and tenants agreed to enclose and apportion 500 acres of open field and 600 acres of heath. The financial gains to the lord of enclosure were indisputable—in 1544 the rents Poure received from the pasture closes were one of his most valuable sources of income.

The majority of Oxfordshire farmers did not enclose during the 17th century but were quite enterprising in their attempts to improve the quality of their farming. In many places the original two open fields had been re-divided or extended into three or four, the last becoming common in the Cotswolds and north Oxfordshire in the early 18th century. New, and more nutritious, crops of clover, trefoil, lucerne, sainfoin, and turnips were introduced to provide better fodder for cattle. In 1638 the lord of the manor of Middleton Stoney, the rector, and tenants agreed 'to lay down for every yardland of the said farm and demesne, 6 acres of grass for every second year in North field, and that every one of the said tenants shall lay down for every yardland which they hold 5 acres for grass yearly in the cornfield'. In this way they, and others like them, turned about a quarter of their land into temporary pasture. The cattle which grazed on it provided the manure to improve its productivity when used again to grow cereal crops.

There were limits to the possible improvement of open-field farming. Time was wasted cultivating dispersed and fragmented holdings and disease spread rapidly among livestock; as one Oxfordshire farmer complained bitterly, 'I have known years when not a single sheep kept in open fields escaped the rot'.

It was usual after 1758 for the lord of the manor, the rector, and other owners of land in a parish to initiate enclosure proceedings and apply for an Act of Parliament. Commissioners were appointed to see that the land was properly surveyed and allotted fairly. The prime movers to enclose at Adderbury in 1768 were the Duke of Argyll and Charles Townshend, grandson of 'Turnip' Townshend. Both had purchased land in the parish over the preceding years and there were already 965 acres of old enclosure. Of the 4,310 acres allotted by the Act, New College received 544 acres. The college let their land as one holding and the rents received from it shortly after show how much more profitable farming could be when the land was enclosed.

Enclosure did not always proceed smoothly but that which caused more trouble than all the others put together concerned Otmoor. It covered about 4,000 acres and from time immemorial the inhabitants of the surrounding seven 'towns'—Charlton-on-Otmoor, Beckley, Noke, Oddington, Fencott, Murcott, and Horton-cum-Studley—had rights of

74

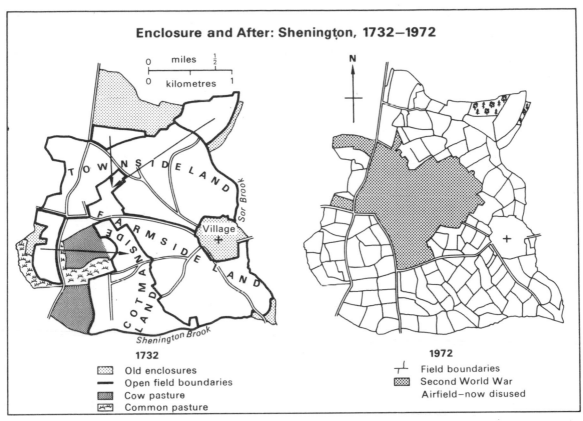

Enclosure and After: Shenington, 1732–1972

0 miles ½
0 kilometres 1

N

T O W N S I D E L A N D

Sor Brook

F A R M S I D E L A N D

Village

C O T M A N L A N D

Shenington Brook

1732
- Old enclosures
- Open field boundaries
- Cow pasture
- Common pasture

1972
- Field boundaries
- Second World War Airfield–now disused

common on it. Here the cottagers, some of them very poor, could eke out a livelihood keeping geese and catching fish and fowl. When the Duke of Marlborough petitioned Parliament for its enclosure in 1801, the men who tried to put up the notices to that effect on the doors of the parish churches, were prevented from doing so by hostile crowds. In 1815 the local landowners tried again and this time an Act to drain and enclose the moor became law. Each of those who had had rights of common was allotted a share of the moor, provided they paid a part of the cost of draining the moor and fenced in their land. Many could not afford to do this and their 'commons' were bought up for £5 each by local land-hungry farmers. In 1829 the diverted river Ray overflowed its new banks for the second time, flooding the best land. Angry farmers cut the new dykes and allowed the river to return to its former course. They were arrested and indicted of felony, but acquitted. This was the signal for the unleashing of all the pent-up feelings of the local inhabitants about the unfairness of enclosure. For the next three years they were in a state of guerilla warfare with the landowners. Men would gather together at night with their faces blackened or veiled in black scarves and armed with

75

*Robert Fowler's
Longhorn*

guns, billhooks, forks, and sticks would set about tearing down fences and uprooting hedges. The landowners seemed powerless to stop them. They employed special constables to watch at night, but their loyalty was suspect; they offered large rewards for information, but none was forthcoming. In 1832 Sir Alexander Croke asked the Government for troops to be sent but his request was refused. Quarter Sessions set up a special committee to deal with the crisis and police were sent from London. In time order was restored, but the story of the struggle of the people of Otmoor against enclosure has become almost legendary.

There remained the Forest of Wychwood whose enclosure was strongly advocated by Arthur Young, not only for agricultural reasons: 'Nor is it in the view of productiveness alone that such an inclosure is to be wished: the morals of the whole surrounding country demand it imperiously. The vicinity is filled with poachers, deer stealers, thieves and pilferers of every kind . . . and Oxford gaol would be uninhabited were it not for this fertile source of crime'. It was disafforested in 1853 and 1856 and in 1862 some 1,500 acres were enclosed and passed to the owner of Cornbury Park. This is all that remains of the vast royal forest which once extended over 102,400 acres. Farmers eagerly took up their shares but found the land very expensive to clear and put into cultivation, and after a series of bad harvests in the 1860s at least one farmer was forced for financial reasons to give up his farm.

The results of enclosure were far-reaching. The most obvious was stated by Arthur Young commenting on farming in north Oxfordshire in 1811, 'the husbandry was incredibly improved in almost every particular'. One farmer in the Redland district was rumoured to be making £20,000 a year from his estate. Rents from land and buildings rose steeply, and great strides were made in improving stock breeding. Robert Fowler of Little Rollright bred high-quality Longhorn cattle, and when the herd was sold in 1791 it reached a very high price. For many enclosure meant hardship and misery. The population was increasing, prices were rising, but the numbers employed on the land were falling. The time when every man had land to cultivate to provide him with food was over for ever. The drift from the land to the industrial towns was well under way. The effects on the landscape were many and extensive. The large straggling open fields were replaced by numerous small fields neatly hedged and fenced. Roads were realigned and the number of farms reduced. Before enclosure many farmers lived in villages and towns at a distance from the land they farmed. When the open fields were enclosed, and holdings were consolidated, it became practicable and convenient for the farmer to build himself a house and live on the land he farmed. The houses vacated, like those improved during the farming boom of the late 16th and early 17th centuries at Little Milton, were divided up into smaller units as cottages for farm labourers. A noticeable feature of the county is the number of isolated farm-houses built in the 19th and earlier centuries, following enclosure.

Christopher Holloway, 1828-95

Profitable farming was, however, short lived. In 1854, after two abnormally wet years, farmers on the clay soils were in such financial straits that they employed fewer men than ever, postponed much needed improvements, and had to use up capital to keep their farms going. The wheat yield that year was 'miserably deficient' and no increase in price could make up the losses. Poor harvests in the 1860s and foreign competition led to a serious depression in agriculture in the 1870s. Rents fell, and it became difficult to get tenants. Farms were amalgamated, buildings left to decay, and land reverted to scrub. The ordinary farm workers were having a hard time and in the 1870s a local branch of the National Agricultural Labourers Union was formed. One of its members was Christopher Holloway of Wootton who took a leading part in pressing local farmers to increase the basic wage of the agricultural labourers from 11s. to 16s. a week. The farmers' reply was to form the Oxford Association of Agriculturists and to resolve not to pay more and not to employ any union man. The farm workers went on strike and 16 women from Ascott-under-Wychwood were sent to prison for assaulting labourers brought in to replace union men. Some workers left the county—40 families from Wootton alone went to find work in Sheffield and many others emigrated. The basic wage was finally raised but only to 14s., and in 1903 workers were being paid only 14s. 11d. a week.

In spite of all the difficulties, there were innovations, experiments, and improvements. The Oxfordshire Agricultural Society, founded in 1811, was one of the earliest societies of its kind to be formed and it did much to improve the standard of stock-breeding and rearing. Robert Hobbs of Kelmscott had an exceptionally find herd of pedigree Shorthorns and did much to encourage better stock keeping. A new breed of sheep—the Oxford Downs—was introduced into north Oxfordshire. The National Land Company, founded in 1845 by Fergus O'Connor, a Chartist, and others, with the aim of settling and re-settling on the land workers from the manufacturing towns, bought 297 acres in Minster Lovell. Most of this was divided up into small holdings of two to four acres. The company failed to raise enough money to pay off the mortgage, and the colony, named Charterville, had to be sold. Some of the tenants chose to return to the industrial towns, but those who stayed made a fair living out of growing potatoes.

77

growing potatoes.

In 1839 the first Royal Agricultural Show was held on seven acres of pasture in Oxford, now the site of Mansfield College. This was long before the railway had been built, and the exhibits and stock took weeks to travel to the show ground. Among the exhibits were a horse-hoe and harrow from Burcot, turnip cutters from Banbury, and a scorcher from Charlbury. The Show was a great success and over 15,000 people visited it. When it was held again in Oxford in 1870 it had grown so much that the Show extended to over 70 acres. Agriculture was still by far and away Oxfordshire's most important industry.

XIV Industrial Pursuits

The manufacture of cloth is, after agriculture, probably the oldest industry in Oxfordshire. Cloth was woven in most families for home use before the Norman Conquest. The Weavers' Gild in Oxford, founded before 1130, was one of the earliest in England. Its success did not last, however, and though cloth was made in Oxford throughout the Middle Ages, it was Witney that became the leading textile centre in the county. Its position on the edge of the Cotswolds—an area renowned for its wool and cloth in the Middle Ages—was ideal. There was a fulling mill there in 969 and by 1278 there were three. The bishop of Lincoln, lord of the manor of Witney, encouraged the keeping of sheep, and in 1278 the clip was recorded as being worth more than the flock.

Blanket Hall, Witney, 1721

The Witney weavers made a broad cloth—the famous blanket cloth —and it brought great prosperity and renown to the town. In 1677 Robert Plot wrote after visiting Witney: 'The blanket trade . . . is advanced to that height that no place comes near it . . . they are esteemed so far beyond all others, that this place has engrossed the whole trade of the nation for this commodity'. In 1711 the Company of Blanket Weavers was formed and among its 114 members was one Thomas Early.

It was still a domestic industry. Most of the spinning and weaving was done by men, women, and children living in the neighbouring villages. In 1768 over 2,000 people, of whom 400 were actual weavers, were working in their own homes for the Witney Gild Masters. A 'good stout woman' could earn 10*d.* to 1*s.* a day spinning; old women 6*d.* a day picking and sorting wool. Each week four or five waggon loads of blankets and duffields, a coarser cloth, made the long journey to London, and from there some of the blankets went to Spain and Portugal and the duffields to North America.

Factories and mechanisation came slowly. The Early family owned four of the six biggest blanket weaving firms in Witney in 1838. John Early's was the largest, employing 70 men. Thomas Early used the fly shuttle for the first time in 1800. Power looms were not installed until the 1850s. They meant the end of weaving as a cottage-based industry and people now had to work in the mills and factories in Witney itself. Though the number employed in the blanket industry fell to as few as 200 in 1807, an expanding market and the introduction

79

W. Bliss & Sons
Textile Mill,
Chipping Norton

of machinery helped to revive trade, and in 1852 the number employed had risen to at least 800.

In and around Banbury, weaving was already a well-established cottage industry when Cobb's factory opened in 1700, specialising in the manufacture of webs, girths, horsecloths, and waggon tilts. The increase in road transport at that time and Banbury's position at the meeting point of several important roads created a great demand for these goods. The firm was a small one, but larger than any other textile business in the area. It closed in 1870, its decline brought about by the increase in rail travel.

In about 1750, weavers in the Banbury region were also making shag or plush, a material made of worsted with hair or silk and having a long velvet nap on one side. Business boomed; in 1831 about 550 men were employed to make this cloth on their own looms, some living 12 miles from Banbury. The cloth was of fine quality and was exported all over southern Europe. Its decline was largely due to the opening of rival firms in Coventry, where the cloth was machine-made. In 1851 the dwindling population of Adderbury was put down in part 'to the removal of several plush weavers with their families to Coventry'.

The Banbury firms tried changing to the manufacture of tweeds, but the scheme failed, and in 1893 there were only 100 full-time textile workers left in Banbury. The last plush factory closed in 1909, selling out to a firm at Shutford, a few miles west of Banbury. Here plush was made for another 40 years, mainly for liveries. Among its customers were the English, Russian, and Danish courts, and foreign embassies.

Chipping Norton's fame as a textile centre came with the establishment in 1746 of Bliss's Mill where webs and horseclothing were made for the extensive coach traffic which passed through the town on its way between Oxford and Worcester. Early in the 19th century the company switched to making serges and tweeds for which it gained a world-wide reputation. The present mill opened in 1872.

In north Oxfordshire many people dressed leather and made gloves, again in their own homes. There were good supplies of raw materials to be had from the sheep, deer and other animals, and a constant demand for leather goods from those who came to hunt or ride in the royal forests. Breeches and jerkins were made at Bampton, and Burford had a European reputation for saddlery. But it was for gloves that the region became best known. They were made in Oxford in the 13th century and there was a Glovers' Gild in 1461. They were also made at Woodstock and during the 16th century it became the centre of the trade in the county. The gloves were cut out in Woodstock by men, from local and imported skins,

23. The Divinity School, designed by master mason Richard Winchcombe and completed in 1490, is a very fine example of 15th-century vaulting.

24. The Bodleian Library, Selden End, looking down through Duke Humphrey's Library, to Arts End.

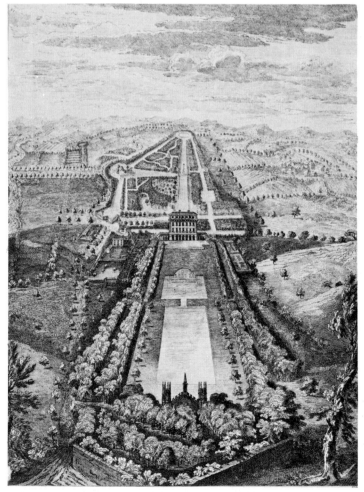

29. *(above)* Chastleton House was built by Walter Jones of Witney and is a beautiful example of an early Jacobean house.

30. *(left)* Shotover House in 1750. The care and attention paid to the laying out of the grounds of large country houses can clearly be seen here.

23. The Divinity School, designed by master mason Richard Winchcombe and completed in 1490, is a very fine example of 15th-century vaulting.

24. The Bodleian Library, Selden End, looking down through Duke Humphrey's Library, to Arts End.

25. The Great Hall, Christ Church, completed in 1529, was the work of Thomas Wolsey for his foundation of Cardinal College.

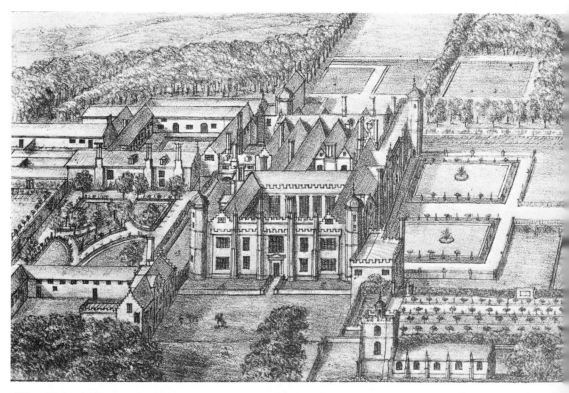

26. Rycote House, the home of Lord John Williams, was destroyed by fire in 1745 and demolished. The 15th-century chapel still stands and has many interesting features including a pew of two stories.

27. North east veiw of Broughton Castle in 1729. It was transformed from a simple medieval building of hall and two wings into an Elizabethan mansion by Richard Fiennes, Lord Saye and Sele.

28. Shirburn Castle was built in 1377 mainly of brick. It has belonged to the Earls of Macclesfield since 1716.

29. *(above)* Chastleton House was built by Walter Jones of Witney and is a beautiful example of an early Jacobean house.

30. *(left)* Shotover House in 1750. The care and attention paid to the laying out of the grounds of large country houses can clearly be seen here.

Industries to 1900

- ■ Cloth-making; *Witney* in production 1973
- ◉ Glove-making; Woodstock in production 1973
- **P** Paper mills; **Wolvercote** in production 1973
- ● Leather work
- ▲ Stone quarrying
- C Clay digging
- ſ Steel
- L Lace
- h Chair leg turning
- ⊖ Brewing
- ▼ Stonesfield slates
- B Brick making
- ⬡ Bell foundries
- ⊗ Agricultural machinery
- ♯ Basket and straw work
- ⊥ Boat building and repairs
- ⊠ Ochre

and then delivered by pack-women to women and girls living in the surrounding villages for making up. Children had to tie the end threads of the fingers because the work required especially small hands. In 1809 over 60 men and 1,400 women and girls were engaged in the work and they made over 360 dozen pairs of gloves a week. The work spread to Charlbury, where the increase in the population between 1841 and 1851 was thought to be the result of an influx of glove

81

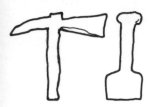

Mason's axe and bolster, Idbury church

workers, and to Witney, Chipping Norton, and Burford, where in 1818 'a person shall be engaged to learn one person in every poor family to make gloves'. But Woodstock kept its lead. Among the orders taken before 1914 was one for 70,000 pairs of strong white leather army gloves, for which the gloveresses were paid 4*d*. or 5*d*. a pair. Gloves are still made in Woodstock.

The excellent stone to be found in north and central Oxfordshire has been used for building from an early date. Banbury was largely constructed of Hornton stone, and Chipping Norton of stone from Pudlicote. Taynton stone was used extensively throughout the county and more especially at Blenheim Palace. The building activities of the colleges and University in Oxford in the 14th and later centuries gave a great impetus to stone quarrying at Wheatley. In the late 16th century nine colleges leased or owned quarries in Headington. Demand was so great that inferior stone sometimes got used by mistake and its poor weathering quality was apparent in the 18th century. Stone was quarried at Wheatley, Taynton, and Headington for use at Windsor Castle, and at Headington and Burford for the rebuilding of St. Paul's Cathedral after the Great Fire of London in 1666. By the mid-19th century the large-scale extraction of stone had ceased; Headington quarries were used only for road stone. The Headington quarries once covered 90 acres and the 'vast rabbit warren of old quarries and tip-heaps' can still be seen even though the area has been extensively built upon in recent years.

During the Middle Ages and later, houses and cottages in north Oxfordshire were often roofed with Stonesfield slates. In the 19th century the stone was quarried underground between Michaelmas and Christmas and then covered over with turves. As soon as a hard frost was likely, the church bells would be rung, and all the menfolk in the village would turn out to expose the stone and lay it out; the frost would then split it ready for shaping. The slates became very popular and many old buildings were stripped and the slates sold for use on new buildings.

In central and southern Oxfordshire bricks were the usual building material. At first they came from Brill in Buckinghamshire, but in 1416-17 kilns at Nettlebed were producing bricks for use at Stonor Park. Clay was in abundant supply and brickworks opened at Woodstock and Caversham (now in Berkshire) in the 17th century. By the 19th century bricks were being made in at least 19 places in the county. Some of the kilns, though now dilapidated, can still be seen. One of the most interesting is at Nettlebed, probably built in the 18th century. Many of the 19th-century brick houses in Didcot and Oxford were built of bricks made in Wheatley.

82

The needs of the University, which had fostered the growth of stone quarrying at Wheatley and Headington, also encouraged a number of specialised trades in Oxford, like bookbinding and parchment making. After 1583-5 when the University Press was finally established, some Oxford people found badly needed employment there. The Press required paper, and with this in mind, Wolvercote Mill ceased to grind corn and began to make paper in about 1672. By 1678 it was producing a fine white paper suitable for use by the Press. In 1718 a contemporary remarked that 'some of the best paper made in England is made at Wolvercote Mill'. Three other corn mills were converted to make paper in the 1680s and several more were established in the 18th century. Eynsham, Sandford, and Hampton Gay mills all made good-quality paper for the University as well as the more common types.

Watermarks of Thomas Quelch of Wolvercote Mill, 1685

Wolvercote was always the most important paper mill in the county. It had a reliable source of water power and coal could be brought to the mill direct from the canal. In 1870 the mill was purchased by the Delegates of the Clarendon Press and it has been owned by the University ever since. The other mills suffered a decline in business during the 19th century—the rising cost of transporting materials and coal became prohibitive. After 1907 only Wolvercote and Sandford Mills remained in use.

Brewing, like paper making, was once widespread. Oxford had several brewers in 1240. At one time nearly every town had its own brewery; those at Oxford, Witney, Banbury, Chipping Norton, Burford, Thame, and Henley were especially good and had impressive buildings, some of which have survived. But no one brewery seems to have employed more than 30 people at any one time.

In the late 18th and 19th centuries small-scale engineering firms opened, mainly producing agricultural machinery. In 1760 W. Lucy and Co. established a wrought iron works at the Eagle Ironworks in Oxford. In 1868 John Allen and Co. were making steam ploughs, rollers, and traction engines at Cowley. In 1865 the Great Western Railway Company wanted to open a large carriage works at Oxford, but opposition from the University was too great and it was established at Swindon instead. In Banbury, James Gardner patented a hay and straw cutter in 1815 and in 1834 a turnip cutter which achieved considerable fame. In 1846 Gardner sold out to Sir Bernhard Samuelson, who made reapers, mowers, and sheaf-binders at the Britannia Works.

In 1886 steam boats were running on the Thames from Salter's boatyard at Oxford. John Salter had set up in business in 1858. Boats were made and repaired at Henley, Goring, and Shiplake.

83

*James Gardner's
turnip cutter*

Many small crafts and trades have been carried on in the county at different times. Banbury was once famous for its cheese which was popular in London during the 16th century. But by the 19th century no one knew how to make it. Towards the end of the 16th century steel was made at Woodstock. It was hand forged from old horse-shoe nails into chains, buckles, buttons, spurs, and scissors and was of good quality. In 1813 a two-ounce chain was sold for £170, but with the development of the steel industry in Birmingham and Sheffield, the craft died out. Church bells were once cast at Woodstock and Burford in the 17th century, and during the 18th century Oxford clockmakers achieved some fame. John Knibb made high quality lantern, 30-hour wall, and bracket clocks.

Lace was made in many Oxfordshire villages, especially those bordering on Buckinghamshire, by the women and girls. But wages were low and when machine-made lace was introduced it became a dying art. Basket-making was once an important craft in and around Thame and Oxford, and the osier beds at Chinnor were still being used in 1918. Hurdles were made from willow and ash poles. In the 19th century men living on or near the Chilterns were making legs for Windsor chairs from the beech trees. In 1853 the industry supported 43 men.

In spite of all these many and varied activities, the choice of work for men, women, and children was never great. Many of them were supplementary employments to help eke out low agricultural wages. None of the industries, not even the textile trades, employed more than a few hundred people. Agriculture was still the main work done in the county in 1902, when an economic historian wrote 'Oxfordshire is prevented, as if by fate, from ever attaining to the position of a great industrial or commercial centre. Oxfordshire is, rather, especially adapted to the requirements and practice of agriculture'. How could anyone possibly know that 20 years later fate would have intervened in the form of the motor car and that consequently Oxford would become a great industrial town?

XV Members of Parliament

In 1290 the king asked that two knights should be chosen to represent the county in his next Parliament. In 1295 he requested that Oxford should send two of its burgesses as well. A few years later some of the smaller towns sent representatives too. Their presence was required to enable the king to raise money. The sending of burgesses was a heavy financial burden on the people who sent them, for they were entitled to the payment of their expenses of 2s. a day while Parliament sat. The city of Oxford and the county could afford this, and were represented consistently, but the smaller towns like Witney, Chipping Norton, Deddington, Burford, and Woodstock soon gave it up. It was so unpopular that in 1453 when New Woodstock received its charter of incorporation the borough was excused from ever again having to send burgesses to Parliament.

Thomas Rowney, jr.

The burgesses from Oxford were chosen by the leading men of the town, which meant the mayor, aldermen, councillors, and freemen. In the county after 1430 the knights of the shire were elected by all forty-shilling freeholders. Throughout the Middle Ages the city was usually represented by its mayor and a leading tradesman. Some must have liked it—Andrew de Pyrie attended 13 Parliaments between 1295 and 1313. The county usually sent the sheriff together with a local man of distinction—Sir John Harcourt elected in 1322 was the first of many from his family to attend Parliament on the county's behalf. Thomas Chaucer of Ewelme achieved fame as speaker of the Commons from 1407 until 1415, and the well-known local families of Wilcote, Stonor, and Quatremaine provided at least one member each.

As Parliament's authority grew the local gentry and nobility came to regard the presence there of men sympathetic to their own particular interests of great importance. Neither city nor county showed any reluctance to exchange their freedom of choice to what amounted to the patronage of one or more of the great magnates. In 1562 the city Council noted that Lord Bedford might choose a burgess for Parliament but that he must send his candidate to be admitted a freeman. During the 16th and early 17th centuries it was customary for the city to elect a member of the Knollys family and in the later 17th century one of the Bertie family. Sometimes their second member was their Recorder or High Steward. Between 1695 and 1759 the two Thomas Rowneys, father and son, represented Oxford.

*Old Town Hall,
1751-1892*

Thomas Rowney junior provided the money to pay for the rebuilding of the Town Hall in 1751-2 and gave the land on which the Radcliffe Infirmary was built.

In 1766-9 the city all but sold one of its seats in return for the payment of the corporation's debts. The Council offered to return unopposed at the next election its existing members provided they paid off the city's debts. If they refused 'the whole council are determined to apply to some other person in the county to do it, and if possible, by that means to keep themselves from being sold to foreigners'. The members refused and reported the matter to the House of Commons. The mayor and his companions were committed to Newgate Prison, but were pardoned a few days later. Undaunted by their experience, the Council opened negotiations with the Duke of Marlborough who showed his willingness to help by paying £6,000 into the city's coffers. Three years later the first of the duke's many nominees was elected to Parliament by the city.

Bribery, which today seems so reprehensible, was an acceptable part of electioneering in the 17th and 18th centuries. Marlborough considered it vital to his cause, 'I think it will be right to give the freemen a treat tomorrow and canvass them for lord Robert (his brother) if possible'. In 1695 Thomas Rowney entertained his voters for £20 and 'they went away civilly', but William Wright's supporters got so drunk that they wandered about the town breaking windows and abusing people. They 'went to Thomas Rowney's house and hooted there and he came out and hooted with them'.

County elections took place in Oxford at the castle, or the Town Hall, or as in 1754 at specially erected booths in Broad Street. In 1709 over 2,600 men voted—there would have been more but for a smallpox scare. From the 16th century onwards there were few local families of note who did not provide a Member of Parliament. The well-known names of Norreys, Chamberlain, Fiennes, Wenman, Cope, and especially Knollys, appear time and time again in the list of county members.

With so many interests to meet, it is not surprising to find that bribery played a large part in county elections too. In 1752 Lord Macclesfield gave a feast for 300 freeholders, and his son was nick-named 'Goody Bribery of Shirburn'.

Elections were not always contested, but that for county representatives in 1754 was long remembered for the campaign launched by the rival New Interest and Old Interest parties. The New Interest, backed by the Duke of Marlborough and the Earl of Macclesfield, supported the Hanoverian and Whig cause, while the Old Interest, with the families of Wenman, Bertie, Dashwood, Lee, and others

86

behind it, were Jacobite in sympathy. From among the large number of electioneering pamphlets and news sheets published during the campaign emerged the *Oxford Journal* which survived afterwards as a weekly newspaper under the proprietorship of William Jackson. It was a costly campaign on both sides. Although the Old Interest candidates received the most votes, the House of Commons on a petition decided in favour of the New Interest.

By the middle of the 16th century the right to send representatives to Parliament had become a much sought-after privilege, and in 1553 it was granted to Woodstock, now eager for the privilege, and to Banbury. Woodstock was allowed to return two members and after the Marlboroughs had been established at Blenheim Palace in the 18th century, it was inevitable that elections would be manipulated in favour of their friends and relations. In 1792 the borough was said to be entirely under their patronage and with 200 people or fewer eligible to vote, it was little better than a pocket borough. Banbury was permitted to return one member and here, by the 18th century, the Norths of Wroxton Abbey had complete control over elections. Between 1754 and 1790 Frederick, Lord North, who was Prime Minister between 1770 and 1782, represented the town. In return the Norths gave generously towards the town's activities. They rebuilt the almshouses, endowed the Blue Coat School, and entertained the corporation lavishly. As the mayor of Banbury remarked, 'most corporations make a considerable advantage of their elections, and they knew no reason why they should not do it as well'.

In 1604 James I decided that the Universities of Oxford and Cambridge should send representatives to Parliament, the right to elect resting with Doctors and Masters of Arts. The University acquired a reputation for supporting the Stuarts, and during the early years of George I's reign, Oxford was known as the 'Jacobite capital of England'. George I's coronation passed almost without celebration, 'the illuminations and bonfires were very poor and mean' according to one eye-witness. On the anniversaries of George I's accession, coronation, and birthday, rioting was not uncommon among students. In 1715 after the king's birthday had been celebrated, hostile crowds gathered shouting 'King James the third! The true king! No usurper', and the students attacked and seriously damaged the Presbyterian, Quaker, and Baptist meeting houses. After the accession of George III the University came to accept the Hanoverians, and in its support of the Anglican church opposed any relaxation of the restrictions imposed on Roman Catholics and Dissenters. When Robert Peel, one of the University's two representatives, decided to support Catholic Emancipation in 1829, he felt he must resign his seat and he was not re-elected.

Frederick, Lord North

Sir Robert Peel

87

Sir Bernhard
Samuelson

The University remained opposed to all religious and Parliamentary reform in the 19th century, including the bills to reform Parliamentary representation, and the Reform Act of 1832 was contemplated with 'sorrow and alarm'. But the county as a whole was in favour of extending the suffrage, reducing the influence of the nobility, and withdrawing representation from depopulated areas. There was considerable excitement and activity in Banbury during the campaign which preceded the election of 1831 and great emphasis was laid on the need to free the town from the North domination.

The Reform Act of 1832 left the University and City representation as before. Woodstock lost a member, while the county gained a third one. The right to vote was extended so that about one man in five was enfranchised. Corruption and bribery remained. During an election of city members in 1857 the result of the contest depended on 40-50 floating voters. Their support was bought by the campaign committee of Charles Neate, one of the four candidates. They employed 198 people as poll clerks at £1 each, paid high rents for committee rooms and for windows from which to hang their flags. They paid people for putting out the flags and others for seeing their rivals did not take them down. In 1880 one of the city's members was unseated for corrupt practices at election time and the vacancy was never filled. In 1885 the city's representation was reduced to one. As late as 1924 Frank Grey lost his seat for corruption during an election. Nonetheless, many men of great distinction represented the city during the 19th and 20th centuries, including Edward Cardwell, Secretary of War, Sir W. V. Harcourt, J. W. Chitty, Lord Chief Justice, and Quintin Hogg, Lord Hailsham, Lord Chancellor. Among the unsuccessful candidates was William Thackeray, the novelist, who contested a bye-election in 1857, and was shocked by the corrupt way in which the campaign was conducted.

Banbury managed to throw off the North domination and elected Henry Tancred in 1831, 'a Whig and something more', who represented the town until 1859. From 1865 until 1885 Sir Bernhard Samuelson, who did so much to improve the educational and industrial opportunities of Banbury, sat as a Liberal. Woodstock remained under the influence of the Marlborough family and from 1874 to 1885 was represented by the 'dashing parliamentary gladiator', the outspoken and fiery Lord Randolph Churchill.

In 1885 Banbury and Woodstock lost their separate representation. At the same time the county was divided into three constituencies, each returning one member. In 1918 it was re-divided into two electoral districts of Banbury and Henley. After long debates over a period of several years the University, along with other universities, lost its

88

right of representation by the Representation of the People Act, 1948. In February 1974, the last General Election before the county boundary was changed, Oxfordshire returned four Members of Parliament, one each for the Banbury, Mid-Oxon, Henley, and Oxford constituencies.

XVI Highways, Waterways, and Railways

Radcot Bridge

So long as people had to travel on foot, they took the easiest route, avoiding marshy ground and too many river crossings. The Icknield Way, with both a winter and a summer route, was one of the earliest trackways in use in the county and it ran along the foot of the scarp of the Chilterns to cross the Thames at Streatley or Wallingford. The Romans with their sophisticated methods of road-making took the direct route irrespective of terrain. It was left to the English to lay down the system of roads which is familiar today in the county, and their work was largely completed before the Norman Conquest. There was an important route from Southampton through Oxford to Northampton, and Banbury Lane which runs from Banbury towards Northampton was mentioned in a 10th-century document. An even more important road ran from London through High Wycombe and Tetsworth to Oxford with branches to Bristol and Gloucester, and was one of a few roads drawn out on a mid-14th-century map.

Road travel out of Oxfordshire was hampered by the lack of bridges over the river Thames. There were ferries at Bablockhythe, Swinford, Sandford, and Caversham, and fords at Oxford. By the 12th century there were bridges at Oxford and Wallingford, at Caversham by the 13th and Radcot by the 14th. However, there were no bridges between Oxford and Wallingford until the 15th century.

There was no organisation to maintain bridges or roads. It was usual for individual lords to see that the roads in their respective manors were kept passable, the actual work being done by tenants. Sometimes the monks, like those at Bicester Priory, repaired the roads near their houses. Occasionally the king allowed the citizens of Oxford to raise a tax for a year or two to repair the road from Oxford through St. Clement's parish. In 1447 a hermit was allowed to collect alms from travellers at Tetsworth for the repair of the road between Stokenchurch and Wheatley. Wealthy men like Lord Williams found the highways a worthy cause. He left £30 for the repair of the footway from Oxford to Botley. Such piecemeal measures fell far short of what was needed and the roads were at best little more than rough tracks, full of potholes, worn into ruts by cartwheels, muddy in wet weather, dusty in dry.

In the mid-16th century the first serious efforts were made by Parliament to rectify this. Each parish became responsible for the

90

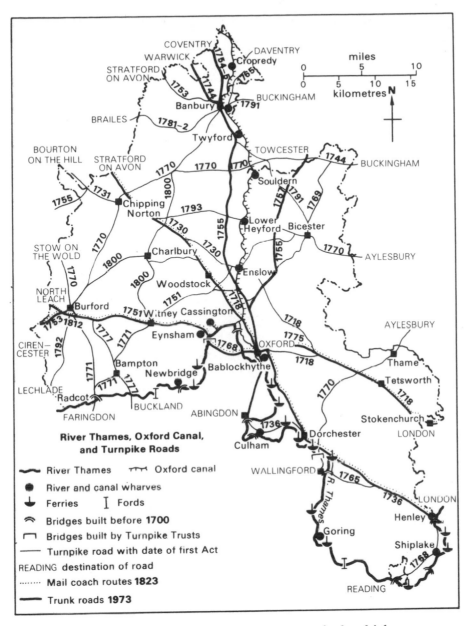

River Thames, Oxford Canal, and Turnpike Roads

- ⌒⌒ River Thames ⊤⊤⊤ Oxford canal
- ● River and canal wharves
- ⊥ Ferries Ⅰ Fords
- ⌒ Bridges built before **1700**
- ⊓ Bridges built by Turnpike Trusts
- — Turnpike road with date of first Act
- READING destination of road
- ⋯⋯ Mail coach routes **1823**
- — Trunk roads **1973**

roads within its boundaries, and surveyors of the highways were appointed by the parishioners. All men had to give materials, carts, and draught animals as well as a few days' labour each year towards keeping the roads repaired. The system failed. In 1576 the roads and bridges leading to Oxford were so decayed from frequent flooding that villagers could not get their produce to the market there without great danger. Men simply did not turn up to do the work, preferring to be fined, and in 1593 they were allowed to compound.

91

Criticism became increasingly vociferous. In 1623 the roads were 'now so worn and broken that in the winter season they are for travellers dangerous'. The surface of the road over Shotover Hill, then part of the route from Oxford to London, was so bad in 1689 that a man's death was 'supposed to be occasioned by his violent motion going up . . . on foot'. In 1725 the way up Headington Hill was 'very rough and uneven, hardly giving passage to horses, coaches, and waggons', and members of the University opened a subscription to pay for the raised footpath which is still in use. Away from Oxford, the roads were even worse. 'There was no stoned road of any kind from Bampton to the neighbouring towns and villages, and travellers were in the habit of striking across the common . . . and finding their way . . . in the best way they could'. Highwaymen were an additional hazard and in 1692 John Bartlet, a carrier, was attacked, wounded, and robbed of £3,000.

In spite of the poor state of the roads, carriers' carts were doing quite well. In 1626 Thomas Egerley was licensed by the Chancellor of the University to go to London once a week. He could charge no more than 1d. for a letter and 4d. a cwt. for parcels. Scholars were to be given preference, and lutes and virginals were only carried by special arrangement. But in 1638 the inhabitants of Milton, Haseley, Tetsworth, and Lewknor complained of the damage done to 'those bad ways' by the four-wheeled carrier-carts, and their use was banned. Egerley lost trade. He could now only carry books, trunks, apparel, light and costly wares instead of the more profitable heavy goods.

In 1667 Anthony Wood travelled from Oxford to London by stage coach. This was a new way of travelling and became very popular. He left Oxford at 4 a.m., spent the night at Beaconsfield, and arrived in London the next day at 7 p.m. Two years later he went in a fly coach and did the journey in the startlingly short time of 13 hours.

But the roads could not stand the wear and tear of coach transport and Turnpike Trusts were set up to improve and finance the repair of the more important routes, raising money from tolls. The Trusts' toll-houses can still be seen at Dorchester, Stadhampton, Witney, and elsewhere. In 1718 the first Turnpike Trust was set up in Oxfordshire to cover the London road from Oxford to Stokenchurch. In 1775 the road over Shotover Hill was abandoned and instead the London traffic followed the same route out of Oxford as today. The road from Oxford through Witney and Burford to Northleach in Gloucestershire was turnpiked in 1751 and a bridge was built to replace the Swinford ferry in 1777. In 1812 a by-pass was built round the south side of Burford to avoid the steep hill. By the end of the 18th century all the more important roads in the county had been turnpiked.

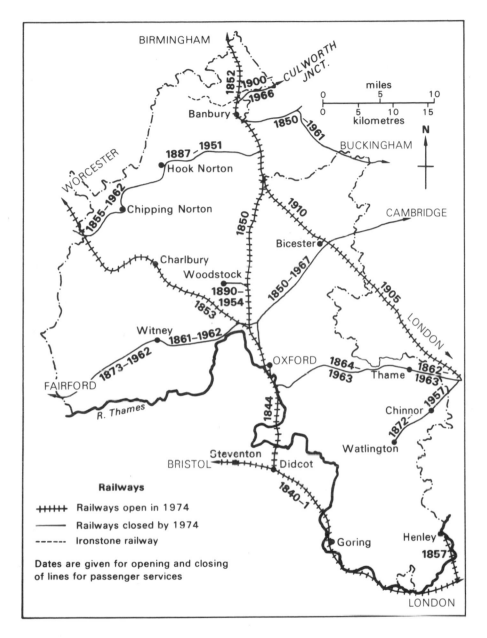

Improvements were slow. In 1769 Arthur Young complained that the 'road from Witney to Northleach is . . . the worst turnpike I ever travelled in, so bad that it is a scandal to the country . . . I travelled it with a very low opinion of all the counties and places it leads to; for if they were inhabited by people of fortune and spirit, I should think they would never suffer such a barbarous method of mending their capital road to subsist'. The roads were made up

Tollhouse,
Dorchester

with stones 'as large as they could be brought from the quarry and when broken left so rough as to be calculated for dislocation rather than exercise'. Forty years later Young was impressed, 'a noble change has taken place'. One result of better roads was the rapid growth of Oxford as a coaching centre. By 1820 some 73 coaches called daily at the excellent inns, like the Angel in the High Street. By 1731 coaches were running from Banbury and, in 1830, 54 coaches a week called there on their way to London and the major towns in the Midlands. Burford, Chipping Norton, and Bicester all enjoyed prosperity as coaching centres. By the middle of the 19th century coach travel was declining, its place being taken by the railways, and most of the Turnpike Trusts had run out of money and were dissolved by about 1878.

The heavy goods that Thomas Egerley could no longer carry in 1638 went to London by the river Thames instead. People living beside its banks had long used it for transporting themselves and their goods. But the navigation of the Thames, especially between Wallingford and Oxford, was fraught with difficulties. In the mid-11th century the merchants of Oxford negotiated with the abbot of Abingdon for a new cut to be made and agreed to pay a toll of herrings every time they used it. In 1316 the abbot and others were accused of constructing locks by which 'ships and boats laden with victuals are unable to pass to the town of Oxford and to return from thence as they have been accustomed to do'. Sometimes boats had to wait several days before a mill owner would allow sufficient water into the river to float the boats. Riparian owners charged exorbitant tolls for letting the boats pass.

In 1605 the first of a series of Acts of Parliament was passed by which the navigation was to be improved so that boats could get up to Oxford and beyond more easily. But in 1611 people complained 'that work does not proceed'. In 1623-4 another Act was passed, and new pound locks were constructed at Sandford and Iffley, but navigation remained unreliable especially in times of flood and drought. In 1714 the river was so low that people could walk across without getting their feet wet, and in 1793 boats were taking up to eight weeks to get from London to Oxford.

The barges carried stone from quarries at Taynton, Burford, and Headington taking it on board at Eynsham, Burcot, or Henley, and delivering it at Windsor or London. Above Oxford the boats carried farm produce and other necessaries. Malt, corn, and timber were shipped from Henley. Boats coming from London sometimes carried unusual cargoes—like the Arundel marbles brought to Oxford in 1667-83. During the Civil War the Parliamentarians did their best

94

to ensure 'that no carriages be conveyed by water to Reading, Oxford, and other places upon the river without a strict search to the end that no victuals, arms, powder, ammunition, or letters of intelligence may be conveyed to the King's army'. Large numbers of barges traded up and down the river from Oxford and in 1812 the Wyatt family had nine working boats.

Grantham's Wharf, Heyford Bridge

Of all the goods that came up the river from London, coal was the most important. It was expensive and in short supply in Oxfordshire because of the long sea and river journey it had to make from Newcastle. There were many in the county like the people of Heyford who 'were greatly distressed for firing, wood being scarce; they were obliged to burn straw etc. or anything they could procure'. Wood was scarce because so many trees had been felled during the Civil War.

It was the promise that the price of coal could be cut from 2s. 2d. to 1s. 4d. a cwt. that aroused so much enthusiasm for a canal from the Midland coalfields to the Thames at Oxford. The promotion meeting held in Banbury in 1768 was attended by the Dukes of Marlborough and Buccleuch, the Lords Spencer, Guilford, and North, members of the University, and the corporations of Woodstock, Banbury, and Oxford, and £50,000 was subscribed on the spot. It took six years to complete the canal from Coventry to Banbury and another 18 to Oxford. The company kept running out of money and by the time the canal was finished £280,000 had been raised. But it was worth the effort and the promise of cheaper coal for Oxford still held good. The first barge to arrive at the New Road wharf in Oxford on 1st January 1790 carried the band of the Oxfordshire militia and was greeted by enthusiastic crowds. The bells were rung, as one church-warden entered in his accounts, 'for rejoicing at ye coals coming to Oxford'. Wharfs were opened up along the canal at places like Cropredy, Heyford, and Souldern for distributing coal.

For 11 years the Oxford canal flourished—it provided the only direct waterway link between the Midlands and London through its junction with the Thames at Oxford. But new canals were being constructed all the time, and faster and more direct routes were being opened up, and traffic on the southern part of the canal declined.

In 1829 the company was still able to pay a good dividend of 32 per cent., but by the end of the 19th century it could only give four per cent. This decline, and that of coach and river transport too, was due to the advent of the railways. In 1833 the Great Western Railway Company produced as part of its plans for a track from London to Bristol, a branch line to Oxford. Opposition to this and later plans was too great. It was claimed the embankments

Oxford Old Station

needed to carry the track back and forth over the Thames would cause flooding. The University opposed it on the grounds that easy travel would undermine discipline among the students and that parents realising this would send their sons to the new universities then being set up. The Turnpike Trusts, the Canal Company, and coach proprietors all foresaw a loss of income. The voices of a few enthusiastic townsmen who hoped for cheaper and more rapid transport of goods and a consequent growth in prosperity were lost.

It was the railway itself which won over most of the opposition. When the London to Bristol line opened in 1840-1, the station at Steventon was only ten miles from Oxford and people from the city made frequent use of it and soon realised the benefits of rail travel and transport. Before the railway was opened it cost £3 to £3 10s. per ton to transport goods from Oxford to London by road and £1 2s. by river. The G.W.R., on the other hand, charged £1 10s. per ton which included the waggon journey between Oxford and Steventon and it took far less time. In June 1844 the line from Didcot to Oxford opened with great celebrations at the station which was then just south of Folly Bridge. This brought a further reduction in the cost of rail transport to a maximum of 12s. 6d. per ton. The station in the Botley Road was opened in 1852 when the line was extended north to Banbury. The L.M.S. station, constructed partly of wood used a year earlier for an entranceway to the Great Exhibition, opened about the same time.

By the end of the 19th century the county was criss-crossed by a network of railway lines, making travel possible for many people who would otherwise seldom have left their own neighbourhoods. The building of some of the lines had caused local disruption. The 150 railroad labourers and their families imported into Cassington to work on the Oxford to Banbury line demoralised the agricultural workers, and the opening of five public houses in such a small place had a bad effect on their habits. Some of the lines should never have been built—that from Princes Risborough to Watlington did not pay through lack of custom, and was never likely to have succeeded. Banbury became an important railway centre, giving the town good communications with the industrial Midlands. But there was no rise in population as in many 19th-century railway junctions, for there was already plenty of spare labour in the town.

Like earlier forms of travel the railways have had their period of decline and many tracks in Oxfordshire have been closed and the lines taken up. However, the river Thames, once so busy with working barges, is now even busier with pleasure craft. The New Road canal wharf was filled in and the site sold for Nuffield College in 1937,

31. Nuneham Courtenay, a view of the flower garden in 1777 from the statue of Hebe to the Temple of Flora.

32. South view of Ditchley Park in 1826 showing the Paladian style house so popular with 18th-century landed gentry. The architect was James Gibbs.

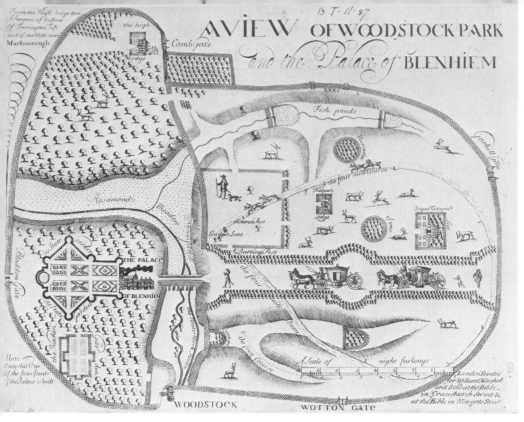

A VIEW OF WOODSTOCK PARK and the Palace of BLENHIEM

33. **Blenheim** Palace was only partly built when this plan of Woodstock Park was made
The race course and other buildings disappeared after the grounds were landscaped.

34. When completed Blenheim Palace covered 7 acres. The grounds were landscaped by Capability
Brown in 1760 when the river was dammed to form a lake. The formal gardens were the work of
M. Duchêre in the 1930s.

and the southern part of the canal was closed to commercial boats in the 1950s. Pleasure cruisers have taken their place too. Roads have come full circle—the demands placed upon them are greater than ever before. The first stretch of road in the county built to Motorway standards opened in 1973 between Stokenchurch and the Waterstock crossroads in Great Milton parish.

XVII   Law and Order

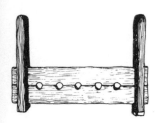

Stocks at Woodstock

In the early Middle Ages the Sheriff was the chief administrative officer in the county. Appointed by the king, he saw that royal commands were carried out, taxes were collected, and that the law was maintained in the county or shire court over which he presided in Oxford. At first the king sent his Itinerant Justices to the county court to record what payments were due to him and to see they were paid. Later they came regularly to hear criminal pleas at what became the assizes. The assize court sat at Oxford Castle until the notorious Black Assize in 1577 when there arose from the gaol there 'such an infectious damp or breath among the people that many there present . . . were then smothered and others so deeply infected that they lived not many hours after'. Six hundred persons sickened in one night and several hundred died. Thereafter, the assize court met in the Town Hall until a new County Hall was built in 1841.

In order to lessen the work of the assize judges, 'keepers of the peace'—the Justices of the Peace—were appointed in Edward III's reign to try certain offences and deal with administrative matters concerning the county as a whole at Quarter Sessions. Oxford, Banbury, Chipping Norton, Henley, and New Woodstock were given the privilege of having their own courts of Quarter Sessions in the 17th century. In 1972 both Quarter Sessions and Assizes were replaced by a new Crown Court held in Oxford.

By the time of the Norman Conquest the county was divided, for judical and fiscal functions, into 14 hundreds. The hundred court held by the Sheriff, or in his absence by the hundred bailiff, nominally met every three weeks. All the lords of the manors within the hundred were expected to attend. Sometimes, however, a village or manor was represented by its priest, reeve, and four best men. At these hundred courts, each village's assessment to taxes was settled, minor infringements of the law were dealt with, and every six months Views of Frankpledge were held to ensure that all men were bound together in groups of ten or twelve to keep the peace, each being responsible for the good conduct of the others in the group. Sometimes the more powerful lords were granted, or claimed, the privilege of holding the View of Frankpledge for their hundreds or manors; the abbot of Eynsham held View at Charlbury

98

and also enjoyed the rights to waifs, to strays, and to hang a thief caught red-handed.

In the hundred, the High or Chief Constable, and in the parish, the Petty Constable, had the responsibility for the general good behaviour of the inhabitants. The position of Petty Constable was an ancient one. His duty was to look after the parish arms, see that law and order were preserved, organise the hue and cry, and deliver certain offenders to the Justices of the Peace. The Petty Constables from Chipping Norton, attending Quarter Sessions in 1687, reported favourably on the state of their town. There were no rogues, drunkards, or poachers; there was no tippling, drinking, or unlawful games; watch and ward were kept and the highways and bridges were in good order. In spite of their onerous and important duties, they were often men of little education as their reports show, 'Itum owre poore are brovided for oure stocks and pound and pillery are in sofishent rapare . . .'. It is a reasonable assumption that most of them did not go looking for trouble.

Bocardo

Sentences meted out in the various courts for felonies and mis-demeanours could be very severe. Hanging was common; minor offenders were punished in the cage, pillory, stocks, or whipping posts, while the sharp-tongued, abusive woman got a turn in the ducking-stool. After 1166 criminals could be sent to the county gaol at Oxford Castle and by 1231 the city, too, had a gaol for its offenders. This was over the Northgate, and by 1318 was called the Bocardo, a name which may be derived from the word bocard or privy. If so, it says much for its condition! All prisoners, male or female, were housed together until about 1310 when after some 15 years' agitation, the Chancellor of the University managed to get the Council to provide a separate room for women, 'the maidens' chamber'. The Chancellor sent offending students to both the city and county prisons. In 1331 when the castle gaol was full, the Constable asked that no student be sent there unless he was 'a common and notorious malefactor'.

Both prisons were dirty, smelly, and overcrowded, and the treatment of prisoners was sometimes harsh. In 1324 the keeper of Bocardo was accused of ill-treating prisoners, and in 1369 he was told not to beat his charges, but to guard them in an honest way. In 1642 the castle prison was used to house prisoners of war. Edward Wirley wrote an account of his experiences while there for the House of Commons. There was no sanitation; they wore rags; and the place was so crowded that even if they had had beds, there would have been no room to lie down on them. In 1688 the castle inmates petitioned the Justices of the Peace about their discomforts. 'We are many in number and

99

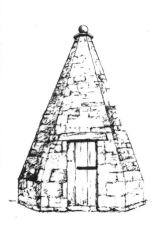

'The Round House',
Wheatley lock-up

miserable poore and have suffered long hardship and tedious imprisonment'. In 1690 a prisoner complained about the keeper's wife, 'a man
had better be subject to slavery than to this woman, for she is the
Devil'. There were frequent petitions for bread from prisoners 'in a
miserable poore condition and in very great want'. In 1777-9 the
prison reformer John Howard visited the prison and found nothing
good to say about it. He thought the rooms used were the same as
those occupied at the time of the Black Assize, and if crowded again
he would not wonder to hear of another fatal occurrence.

Conditions at Bocardo were no better. In 1605 the prison consisted
of a dungeon, close room, women's ward, and freemen's ward with
an inner ward. Freemen debtors were allowed to beg from passers-by
by lowering a bag out of the window for people to put their gifts in.
Among the prison furniture in 1754 were stocks, fettering irons,
collars, shackles, 11 pairs of fetters, five pairs of handcuffs, and two
thumbscrews. Bocardo was demolished along with Northgate in
1770-1, and a new town prison was built at Gloucester Green. It was
considered good when opened in 1789, but in 1836 it was so damp
that the bedding was wet, and there was no heating and little ventilation. In 1857 the Inspector of Prisons said it should be rebuilt or the
prisoners sent to the castle. It was finally closed in 1878, and demolished. The county gaol, on the other hand, was greatly enlarged and
improved during the 19th century and the Justices who administered
it did so competently. The last public execution took place there
in 1863. The prison was still in use in 1973.

Outside Oxford there was a small gaol at Banbury after about 1558
until the mid-19th century. In 1851 the Inspector of Prisons said
it was the worst prison he had ever seen. The Town Council tried
to build a new one but was unable to raise the money. There were
similar small prisons at Thame and Witney in the 18th century and
many places had a lock-up where people could be held before being
taken to the Justices.

Until the 19th century there were no police forces. In the Middle
Ages when a crime was committed all the inhabitants in the neighbourhood had to join the hue and cry in pursuit of the offender. The
Petty Constables and watchmen were supposed to keep order and
bring offenders to court. In 1756 an advertisement in a local paper
suggested that gentlemen and tradesmen in Oxfordshire should join
together for the discovery, punishment, and prevention in the future, of
all murders, robbery, theft, and unlawful invasion of anyone's property.
If a large peace-keeping force was needed there was no alternative to
calling out the military. This was done in Banbury on several occasions,
and in 1800 when troops charged a mob a child was killed.

100

Keeping the peace in Oxford was especially difficult. The University acquired the right of policing the streets at night and forbade any townsman to be out at night without good cause. In 1609 the town bailiffs were each fined £20 for breaking the curfew. When the Council set up a police force in 1835 after the London model, it was allowed only to patrol the streets during the day, the University maintaining a quite separate night force. This made efficiency virtually impossible. In 1868 the University and city agreed upon a united force to be financed and controlled jointly. Complete control was not given to the city until 1889. During the latter half of the 19th century it was praised by the Inspectors of Constabulary for being well run.

Banbury formed a police force in 1836. Here, as in Oxford, discipline was difficult to maintain and there were many and frequent dismissals for being drunk on duty, insubordination, and lateness. In 1925 the force was amalgamated with the county police which had been set up in 1857. The county and city forces, together with those of Berkshire, Buckinghamshire, and Reading were united in 1968 as the Thames Valley Police Force with headquarters at Kidlington.

XVIII   The Poor and Needy

Porch to Ewelme almshouses, the earliest use of brick in southern England

There have always been people unable to provide for themselves or their families. In the Middle Ages widows with young children, orphans, the sick, aged, and incapacitated were cared for by the people among whom they lived. Vagrancy became an additional problem in Oxfordshire towards the close of the 15th century. Men who fell out of work, and many families who lost their homes as a result of the conversion of arable land to pasture, had little alternative to becoming beggars, 'wandering about and seeking their bread elsewhere'. A few of the aged or sick poor might find shelter in one of the almshouses founded by a religious gild or local benefactor. Richard Quatremaine and his wife founded an almshouse for six poor men at Thame in 1447 and William and Alice de la Pole, Duke and Duchess of Suffolk, one for 13 poor men at Ewelme in 1437.

In 1601 the responsibility for the relief of the poor was laid on the parish vestries. They had to choose overseers of the poor who would administer the relief considered necessary, usually food, clothes, and fuel. They repaired houses, apprenticed boys and girls, paid for burials and lying-in, and for medicines and doctors. When a poor man died at Wigginton in 1734 the parish paid 10s. for his coffin, 1s. for his laying-out and for ale at his funeral, and 1s. 4d. for ringing the bell and digging the grave. There were few places that did not have at least one charity by which additional gifts of money, bread, or fuel could be made at Christmas or Easter, and lists of bequests are often to be found in parish churches. Many more almshouses were founded during the 17th century like that at Witney, established by John Holloway, a successful clothier, for six poor blanket-weavers' widows, or at Chipping Norton in 1640 by Henry Cornish for eight poor people. But there were always indignities to be suffered. At Banbury the vestry threatened to withhold relief from those who refused to wear the pauper's badge.

By 1636 Oxfordshire had ceased, for some inexplicable reason, to be one of the wealthiest counties in England, and bad harvests and high prices brought severe hardship late in the 17th century. In 1693 mobs gathered in Banbury, Chipping Norton, and Charlbury demanding cheaper bread. In Oxford angry women pelted the unpopular millers and bakers with stones because of the high prices of flour and

102

bread. Even the socially unaware Anthony Wood noted in 1694 that 'divers starved to death in Oxford'.

There was a growing belief that many of the poor were idle and dissolute and did not want to work. Houses of Correction were opened in Witney and Banbury in 1611-12 and in Thame in 1707, where all rogues, vagrants, and idlers were to be made to work.

The Old Workhouse, Banbury

The problem of how to cope with the growing number of poor was a vexing one. It was also becoming a heavy financial burden on ratepayers. In 1582 Oxford City Council ordered all people who had come to the town in the previous three years to leave unless they could show that they could support themselves. The Laws of Settlement, introduced in an endeavour to help over-burdened parishes, required that every person coming to live or work in a parish must have a certificate stating where he was legally settled—his place of birth or the parish where he had been apprenticed or had worked for a certain number of years. Then if he became chargeable on the Poor Rate he could be sent back there. It was a harsh law, and instead of saving money the overseers went to great expense to prove poor people were not their concern, and to get rid of as many of them as possible. There were other more subtle ways of removing people who might become chargeable. In Witney between 1760 and 1818 the overseers arranged for 97 poor children to serve their apprentice-ships outside the town compared with 29 allowed to remain. At Finmere in 1826 the vestry offered £2 to every young man who hired himself to a master outside the parish.

During the 18th century many overseers opened workhouses to accommodate the sick, aged, and impotent poor and to put some at least of the able-bodied poor to work. In Banbury the overseers arranged with one Richard Burrowes in 1707 that he would employ up to 50 paupers, aged between eight and 60 years, to work in worsted manufacture. Burrowes was to pay them a wage, provide clothing and diet sufficient to keep them from becoming chargeable. He was also to provide materials to employ in their own homes any poor sent to him by two Justices of the Peace and pay them wages. At Wigginton in 1785, Thomas Wilkes, woolcomber, undertook to feed and clothe the poor, nurse the sick and bury the dead for £67 5s. a year plus their free labour. The poor's labour was in fact being farmed, or rented out, to the highest bidder—a common practice at that time.

Towards the close of the 18th century the number of poor seeking assistance increased alarmingly. By 1803 out of every 100 people in the county, 20 were in receipt of aid of some kind. Enclosure caused a lot of poverty—the poor were supposed to be allotted land

103

*Chipping Norton
almshouses*

in place of their rights of common, but this was seldom enough even to make up for the loss of fuel or grazing. The number of workers needed on the new farms fell and many families were left without homes or work. The Settlement Laws made it difficult for the unemployed to seek work elsewhere. The textile trade was going through a bad patch, and when Arthur Young visited Witney in 1768 he found the town 'was threatened with the utter loss of every means of giving bread to its numerous poor'. When he returned in 1809 trade had revived but 'the masters and fabrics may flourish but it cannot be said that labouring hands do the same', for the number employed had fallen from 500 to 140. So desperate were some people that they resorted to extreme measures. In 1797 the inhabitants of Deddington seized a canal boat laden with flour and only let the miller have it back when he agreed not to send the boat out of the county to the Midlands where it would have fetched an inflated price, but to sell it to them at a reduced rate.

At the end of the Napoleonic Wars in 1815, the problem became even more serious. The population was increasing, wages were low, and prices were high. The Poor Laws were quite inadequate and the situation was rapidly getting out of control. The Poor Rates trebled—at some places it was 10s. in the £. At Wigginton the cost of looking after the poor rose from £45 10s. in 1779 to £650 in 1819. A number of different schemes were tried. Some overseers supplemented a man's wage when it fell below a certain level, but even then it was not enough to keep a poor man and his family. In 1795 a Banbury widower with three children earned £21 a year and received £5 4s. from the parish. His bread bill alone came to £13 13s. a year, and it is not surprising to find him in debt for £5. Other overseers adopted the Roundsman system and made the local farmers employ the poor labourers in turn. At Bodicote the unemployed worker was given a printed form which he took with him round the local farmers who signed their names if they could not give him any work. At the end of a jobless day the overseers paid him the equivalent of a day's wage less 2d. At Deddington during the winter months, when farm work was especially scarce, about 60 men applied for employment each day. There was nothing to encourage the labourer to work hard as the overseers of Enstone pointed out: 'The wages they receive will not support them properly to hard work. When a man has worked hard all day, to come home at night to potatoes and bread, it lingers him along; it is not living'.

The number of poor people in Oxford caused many a serious headache. As the preamble to the Act of Parliament which completely reorganised the Poor Law administration in 1771 in 11 city parishes

104

stated, 'the Poor in the city of Oxford are very numerous, and are maintained at a great Expense . . .'. A Board of Poor Law Guardians was set up with representatives from each of the 11 parishes, and in 1775 they opened a new workhouse in Wellington Square 'a very neat building' of two storeys. The 200 inmates were nearly all women, children, and old men. In 1797 it was exceedingly dirty and ill-managed. At times of especial hardship the Board were unable to do more than assist the most needy. During the bad winter of 1794-5 a subscription was opened so that bread could be bought and then resold to the poor at a reduced price. Only the aged poor and those with two or more children and earning less than 12s. a week benefited. Even so 4,200 'necessitated people' were helped, over a third of the city's population. In 1800 the Council instructed the Town Clerk to write a piece for the *Oxford Journal* recommending that people should abstain from using butter while the price was so high.

A lodge, Thame Union Workhouse

Reform for the rest of the county came in 1834. All the parishes were relieved of their thankless task; instead, the county was divided into eight Poor Law Unions, each under a Board of Guardians representative of each parish in the union. Out-relief was to be discouraged; all who sought help were to go into the new union workhouses at Banbury, Witney, Chipping Norton, Thame, Henley, Woodstock, Headington, and Bicester. The Oxford Board opened a new workhouse in the Cowley Road in 1865 next to the Industrial School for poor children.

The workhouse regime was rigorous and unfeeling in order to discourage as many people as possible from seeking aid unless it was absolutely necessary. Once in the workhouse, the poor were segregated according to age, sex, and state of health. Husbands were separated from their wives, children from their parents. All the able-bodied had to work, usually on the roads. The diet was dull and monotonous. So hard and comfortless were the workhouses, that many of the poor preferred to die of cold or starvation than enter their doors. The Poor Rates may have fallen but the misery of the poor did not. Emigration increased. Fifty people went to North America from Deddington, and many others to New Zealand.

The workhouses closed their doors in 1929. Chipping Norton and Cowley Road workhouses are now hospitals; Thame an agricultural college, and Witney an engineering works. Widely different though their present purposes are, their distinctive style of architecture is a reminder of a time when to be a pauper was untold misery.

XIX Houses and Families

Sir John de Broughton

Oxfordshire houses, whether stately homes or farm cottages, were built of local materials. Wood, stone, flint, and clay for bricks were plentiful. Whole villages were constructed of a particular material giving them an air of individuality and homogeneity.

The most important secular building in any village was the manor house and there are many in the county of architectural interest and beauty. It is sad that the manor house at Woodstock, built by the medieval kings of England, was demolished when the grounds of Blenheim Palace were laid out in the 18th century. Although no one knows what it looked like, it was evidently a building of some size and grandeur. During the reigns of Henry II and Henry III the house was always being repaired, altered, and embellished. Henry III alone spent £3,300 on it. By 1272 there were extensive royal apartments and kitchens, six chapels, and a canopied throne in the hall. In 1634 this hall was described as a 'spacious church-like Hall, with two fayre isles, with six Pillars, white, and large, parting either isle'.

Most medieval manor houses were, however, comparatively simple buildings. The original Stonor Park, constructed shortly after 1280 by Sir Richard Stonor for himself and his bride, consisted of an aisled hall, a two-storeyed service wing, and a detached chapel. Broughton Castle, built before Sir John de Broughton died in 1315, had a large hall flanked by two wings, one containing the lord's apartments and the other the kitchens. In 1405-6 Sir Thomas Wykeham, to whom the house had descended, received a licence to crenellate it, although it was never primarily a defensive structure.

During the 16th century it became fashionable, for those who could afford it, to enlarge and refurbish their manor houses. Broughton Castle was transformed, largely by Richard Fiennes, Lord Saye and Sele, to whom it then belonged, from a medieval fortified manor house into an Elizabethan mansion. Rooms were redecorated and remodelled and new ones added in the style of the day. At Stonor, an Elizabethan style front was built to conceal the medieval buildings. Many new and more splendid houses were built. At Mapledurham, Sir Michael Blount, a Sheriff of Berkshire and Oxfordshire, and Lieutenant of the Tower of London, built a new brick house about 1585 to replace the small, out-of-date existing manor house. Alexander Pope was a frequent visitor here in the early 18th century and was a close friend of Martha and Teresa Blount. They feature in his poems, and Pope left Martha some of his books, money, and other belongings.

Kelmscott House in western Oxfordshire, built in stone about 1570, was on a much smaller scale but just as beautiful, 'a gem of late sixteenth century architecture'. In 1871 it was purchased by William Morris, the Victorian poet, artist, designer, and interior decorator, who restored and furnished it with his own wall papers, carpets, and fabrics, most of which are still in the house.

The old manor house, Mapledurham

Chastleton House was built a little later, by Walter Jones, a successful clothier from Witney. He bought the estate from Robert Catesby, forced to sell to pay the fines imposed on him for intrigues and plots against Queen Elizabeth. Jones completed the house in 1614 and it stands today much as it did then. The Great Chamber and Long Gallery are particularly beautiful rooms with panelled walls and moulded plaster ceilings. Arthur Jones, one of its later owners, was a Royalist during the Civil War and Commonwealth and fought at the battle of Worcester in 1651 for the future Charles II. Cromwell's men, under the impression he was the Prince, pursued him to his home where he hid in a secret room. His wife saved his life by drugging the soldiers who planned to stay on guard all night, allowing him to escape while they slept.

Not far away, at Minster Lovell manor house, Francis Lovell sought safety during an earlier civil war. He was created Viscount Lovell in 1483 and served Richard III faithfully, fighting for him at the battle of Bosworth Field. Four years later he fought at the battle of Stoke in an attempt to overthrow Henry VII and was never seen or heard of again. In 1728 a skeleton was found inside a secret room at Minster Lovell manor house, and it may be that Francis hid there to avoid arrest only to starve to death when the sole person who knew he was there and could bring him food or let him out died suddenly. The house was sold to Sir Edward Coke in 1602, but early in the 18th century the Coke family moved to Holkham Hall, Norfolk, and the buildings were left to decay. Now only the ruined walls stand of what must once have been a large and splendid house.

Many men gained from the dissolution of the monasteries, and in Oxfordshire John Williams led the field. He was an astute man who served in turn Henry VIII, Edward VI, Mary, who created him Lord Williams, and Elizabeth. He acquired Thame Abbey, which had been greatly enhanced shortly before it was surrendered by the addition of some new abbot's lodgings, a beautiful example of early Tudor workmanship. When Lord Williams died the abbey passed to his daughter, Isabella, the wife of Sir Richard Wenman. The Wenmans

107

*Pope's tower,
Stanton Harcourt*

were wealthy wool merchants from near Witney. In 1745 all the monastic buildings, except the abbot's lodgings, were demolished and in their place a west front in the then popular Palladian style was added.

Lord Williams did not live at Thame Abbey, for in 1542 he purchased a new and magnificent brick house at nearby Rycote. This house was probably built by Sir John Heron, treasurer to Henry VIII, and his son, to replace an earlier one. Here in 1554 Princess Elizabeth stayed when on her way from the Tower of London to Woodstock manor, where she was kept a prisoner for six months. He must have endeared himself to her, for when she became queen, he was created Lord President of the Council of the Marches of Wales. Rycote passed to his daughter, Margaret, wife of Henry Norreys, and it was their descendant who was created Earl of Abingdon in 1682. Tragedy struck the family in 1745 when the ten-year-old heir died in a fire which severely damaged the house. The family could not bear to stay at Rycote after this and moved to Wytham. Most of what remained of the house was demolished. The 15th-century chapel, with its extraordinary two-storeyed pew and other magnificent woodwork, remains.

Lord Williams's third house in Oxfordshire was a hunting lodge at Beckley. It stands between the inner and middle of three moats of an earlier building. The brickwork is beautifully diapered with black headers and there were three garde robe flues in the projecting back gables.

However active these owners were during the 16th and 17th centuries, they were nothing compared with those of the 18th century. Country houses of considerable size and grandeur standing in extensive parks or landscaped gardens became the vogue. Ditchley House was completely rebuilt in 1722 by the Earl of Litchfield in the Palladian style. Shotover House was built a little before this of Headington stone by General James Tyrrel and his father, whose family had acquired the land after Shotover was disafforested in 1666. Kirtlington Park followed in 1742-6 for Sir James Dashwood, High Sheriff of Oxfordshire and High Steward of Oxford. He inherited a very considerable fortune and the existing family home was no longer thought suitable for a man of his standing. In 1753 Horace Walpole 'passed by Sir James Dashwood's, a vast new home, situated so high that it seems to stand for the county as well as for himself'. Middleton Park and Heythrop House were also built at this time.

In 1711 the Harcourt family decided to leave their old house at Stanton Harcourt where they had lived for six centuries, and to build a new and fashionable mansion at Nuneham Courtenay, splendidly situated on a hill overlooking the Thames. The old house was partly pulled down and the stones used in the new house, but the kitchen, gatehouse, and Pope's tower were left. The kitchen is huge, measuring 33 feet by 31 feet and 64 feet high in the centre, and dates from the late 14th or early 15th centuries. The roof, constructed in 1485, is in the form of an octagonal lantern with slats opening to let the smoke out. The tower got its name from Alexander Pope, who lived there in 1718-19 while working on his translation of the *Iliad*. The new Harcourt residence, finished about 1760, was erected on the site of a village which was completely removed and rebuilt about one and a half miles away, the new cottages and inn flanking the Oxford to Dorchester road. On the whole the villagers were not unduly distressed by this, though the rector was upset about having to move his plants and shrubs. It may have been the old village of Nuneham that Oliver Goldsmith had in mind when he wrote *The Deserted Village*. Walpole liked the house, 'not superb but so calm, *riant*, and comfortable, so live-at-able; one wakes in the morning on such a whole picture of beauty'.

William Kent's Arcade, Rousham

Inside, these houses were decorated elaborately; ceilings were painted with classical and other scenes; fireplaces had ornate mantels, and the walls were hung with portraits of the owners and their families. Outside, the grounds were laid out to add dignity to the houses and owners alike. Long avenues of trees were planted, sometimes over two miles long; artificial lakes were made and summerhouses, grottoes, and even artificial ruins were erected. The gardens of Rousham House are of particular interest for they are the only unspoilt example left of the work of William Kent. He was employed in the 18th century by General James Dormer to bring up to date the Jacobean house both within and without. Walpole was ecstatic about the gardens, 'the garden is Daphne in little, the sweetest little groves, streams, glades, porticoes, cascades and river imaginable; all the scenes are perfectly classic'.

A few of the large houses became scientific and cultural centres. Owners collected fine libraries and became patrons of the arts. Shirburn Castle, built in 1377, and extensively altered in the 18th century, was purchased in 1716 by Thomas Parker, Earl of Macclesfield. He and his son were both interested in scientific research. In 1739 the earl built an astronomical observatory and in 1752 was President of the Royal Society. During the early part of the 17th century the home of Lucius Carey, Lord Falkland, at Great Tew was frequented by many scholars and literary men, including Ben Jonson, Cowley, and John Selden.

In 1705 music, morris dancing, and 'about a hundred buckets, bowls and pans filled with wine, punch, cakes and ale' accompanied the laying of the foundation stone of the county's largest and best-known stately home—Blenheim Palace. The manor and park of

109

*Victory Column,
Blenheim Palace*

Woodstock extending to over 2,000 acres, were granted in 1704 to John Churchill, Duke of Marlborough, by the queen in acknowledgement of the great service he had done his country in defeating Louis XIV of France at the battle of Blenheim. A grateful Parliament granted him money to build a great mansion, not only as a country home for himself and his family, but also as a national monument to the victory. The architect was Sir John Vanbrugh and the resulting Palladian-style building, with a frontage of 800 feet and covering in all seven acres, is both ostentatious and impracticable. The house was not completed until after Marlborough had died, and at one time it looked as though it never would be, for work stopped when the duke fell from power in 1712 and Parliament refused to grant any more money. There were constant rows and bickerings between the duchess and Vanbrugh which held up the work, and when the duke died leaving £10,000 a year to the duchess to complete the building, Vanbrugh remarked bitterly, 'to spoil Blenheim in her own way'. Relations between the two were so bad that when Vanbrugh tried to show the house to some friends he was refused admission. Although Vanbrugh was dismissed before the house was finished, it was built and furnished almost entirely to his specifications. The main entrance to the house and grounds was under Nicholas Hawksmore's triumphal arch. In about 1760 Capability Brown, the landscape artist, set to work to lay out the grounds. The dukes of Marlborough and other members of the family have exerted considerable influence upon the county and the city of Oxford. They have served as High Stewards, High Sheriffs and M.P.s, vying with other local leading families for dominance. After the first duke, the most important member of the family was Sir Winston Churchill who was born at Blenheim in 1874 and buried at Bladon.

The building of large country houses continued into the 19th century. The early 18th-century house at Heythrop was destroyed by fire in 1831 but was rebuilt along the same lines in 1870. Wyfold Court, in south Oxfordshire, a grand and most elaborate house built in the French Late Gothic style, was erected in the 1870s for Edward Hermon, a Lancastrian, who had made his money in the cotton mills.

Some of these houses have remained the property of private individuals, some of them descendants of the original owners. But Nuneham Courtenay is now a college of education; Ditchley House is an Anglo-American conference centre; Wroxton Abbey is part of an American University. Wyfold Court became a mental hospital. The dining-room from Kirtlington House was sold to the Metropolitan Museum of Art in the United States of America. Better this perhaps than that these handsome relics of an age of elegance and gentle living should be destroyed like so many of their predecessors.

110

XX   *The Modernisation of Oxford*

Oxford, that had suffered an economic depression for two and a half centuries, was by 1550 once more a thriving town. It was sharing in the general prosperity experienced all over England at that time which lasted up to the outbreak of the Civil War. The city was dependent for its livelihood to a very large extent on the University and at this time the University was expanding and the colleges were putting up new buildings; the building trades flourished. This dependence was not good for the city, but the Council was too weak, ineffective, and corrupt to break free.

Oxford City arms

Until 1835 when local government was reformed, the Council was made up of about 130 aldermen and councillors elected by 1,400 or so freemen. Much money, time, and effort was spent in trying to prevent any further loss of privileges to the University. Endless, and fruitless, arguments took place about the order of precedence in processions. The Council insisted on protecting the freemen traders from outside competition by maintaining the old, and now out-of-date, gild regulations. They looked after their property, Portmeadow, and their fishing rights. They administered charities, assisted the poor, and tried to keep the streets, rivers and water-courses clean.

Some councillors tried to serve the city faithfully, but during the Civil War of the 17th century their position was undermined at one time by the king's and at others by Parliament's interference. In 1648 nine councillors were ejected by order of the House of Commons for their Royalist sympathies, and after the Restoration 41 were dismissed for having supported Parliament. In 1681 the Council was forced to accept the king's nominee as Town Clerk, and in 1688 James II demanded that 28 councillors be replaced by men of his choosing. With all this interference, it is not surprising to find in the 18th century that the Council was granting the freedom of the city, with all its privileges, to anyone who might be of assistance to them in local affairs. Council elections became rowdy; bribery was extensive. By 1832 it was customary for the Town Clerk to issue tickets to public houses in Oxford at election time for the dispensing of free liquor to freemen. Many of the more responsible freemen stayed away from elections, because of drunken and disorderly behaviour. In the confusion of the poll, which was taken by the freemen being

111

counted as they passed through a narrow doorway, many voted who were not eligible.

The Municipal Reform Act of 1835 went some way towards rectifying matters. The new Council consisted of ten aldermen and 30 councillors, elected by some 3,000 ratepayers. A sheriff was to be chosen to look after Portmeadow for the freemen, and all trade restrictions were abolished—anyone who wished could now open a shop and manufacture goods to sell in Oxford. But the Council's powers were few, for 'nothing in the Act contained shall be construed to alter or affect the Rights and Privileges Duties or Liabilities, of, . . . the University of Oxford'. It continued merely to administer its property and water supply and to provide a day-time police force.

The position of the University in town affairs made the development of local government quite different from that in other towns, with the exception of Cambridge. In 1771 the Oxford Paving Commissioners were established by Act of Parliament and they included representatives from both the Council and University. They were responsible for widening, improving, lighting, and cleansing the streets, for which they were given extensive powers and the right to levy rates. In 1865 their duties were taken over by the Local Board of Health set up to improve the sanitary condition of the city. This body, too, included members of Town and Gown, although their authority extended beyond the city boundaries to cover some neighbouring parishes. By 1888 there were in Oxford a bewildering number of governing bodies—the Council, the Local Board of Health, the Poor Law Guardians, set up in 1771, a School Board, special committees to run the market and the police force, on all of which the University was represented except the Council, and after 1870 a Volunteer Fire Brigade.

In 1889 the Oxford Order created the city a county borough with greatly extended boundaries and the Council became the main governing body. All the boards and committees, except the Poor Law Guardians, were abolished and their functions taken over by the new city Council of 49 councillors, nine of whom were elected by the University, and 17 aldermen, three of whom represented the University. In this way Oxford was brought into line with other towns, save for the anomaly of University representation which lasted until April 1974.

As a result of working together to improve the city's amenities for the benefit of both University and city, relations between Town and Gown were now so much better that the two could be expected to act in harmony. Feelings had also been improved by the abolition in 1825 of the St. Scholastica's Day penance and in 1859 of the mayor's oath to preserve the rights and privileges of the University.

112

35. W. S. Hitchman & Co.'s brewery at Chipping Norton in about 1860 was one of many in Oxfordshire at that time.

36. Culham brickfield in 1890. The clay was dug locally, the bricks fired in the kiln, and later transported by road, rail, and river.

37. Bobbin winding at Witney blanket mills in 1898.

38. 'Tentering' in 1898. The blanket cloth had to be hung out to dry after being washed.

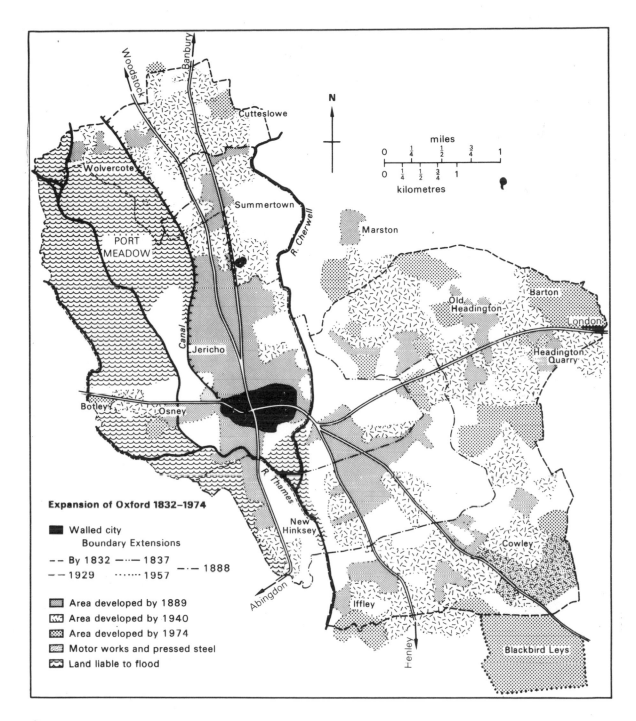

Expansion of Oxford 1832–1974

■ Walled city
   Boundary Extensions

-- By 1832 --·-- 1837
            -- -- 1888
-- -- 1929 ······· 1957

▨ Area developed by 1889
▨ Area developed by 1940
▨ Area developed by 1974
▨ Motor works and pressed steel
≋ Land liable to flood

The city which the various councils and boards governed changed
beyond recognition between the 16th and the opening of the 20th
centuries, although improvement came only slowly and painfully.

Carfax Conduit

The Council was largely ineffective in its attempts to keep Oxford's streets tidy and its rivers clean. They tried without success in 1582 to stop householders from letting swine roam the streets, or from throwing, 'donge, dust, ordure, rubbish, carreyne in any streets, wayes or lanes'. Their request that 'all privies and hogsties set or made over, uppon, or adioyninge to any waters . . . leading to any brewhouse . . . be removed' was largely ignored. From time to time a scavenger was paid for by a tax on all householders to go round and collect refuse and men were paid for sweeping Carfax and Northgate. Most of the town was in darkness at night, though freemen were asked in 1614 to hang a lantern outside their homes during the winter evenings. Most of the streets had no firm surface—gravel was renewed only when the dirt, filth and potholes made it absolutely necessary. It was then up to the householders to see the work was done.

Water for all purposes came from wells or rivers, both heavily polluted. In 1610 Otho Nicholson offered to pay for the conveyance of water in lead or wooden pipes from springs on Hinksey Hill to cisterns at Carfax. The conduit, completed in 1617, had an upper cistern for use by the University and a lower one for the town, and was a splendid and elaborate affair. The colleges made good use of the supply and pipes were laid along the High Street as far as Magdalen College. But demand outstripped supply, and in 1694 the Council set up its own waterworks at Folly Bridge, and elm pipes carried the water to a cistern at Market Hill. The water was untreated and impure, partly because its inlet lay below a sewage outlet.

The Paving Commissioners carried out the first real improvements in the city. They opened up the approaches by rebuilding Magdalen Bridge, then 'in a decayed and ruinous state' and only 13 feet wide in places, and by demolishing Eastgate and Northgate. Botley causeway had already been raised and widened and New Road was opened in 1770. A special Act of Parliament allowed for the rebuilding of Folly Bridge and the charging of tolls to help pay for it. In 1786 Carfax Conduit was removed, for it had become a major obstacle to the growing number of coaches in the city. The crossroads were further improved in 1896 by the city Council when all but the tower of St. Martin's church was demolished. The market was moved off the streets in 1774 to its present site. The main streets were widened and the surfaces made up, at first with stone or gravel, but after 1865 increasingly with tarmacadam. The Commissioners provided oil lamps in the main streets until 1835, when they changed to gas lighting. Measures were taken for the regular removal of refuse—in 1771 householders were told to throw their rubbish into the road between midnight and 4 a.m. twice a week and carts went round to collect it.

The city was an unhealthy place. After a series of outbreaks of smallpox, fever, and plague in the late 17th century, Anthony Wood reluctantly remarked 'Oxford is no good aire'. For hundreds of years the sick were cared for in their own homes or in temporary pesthouses or hospitals. Oxford's first permanent hospital was built by the Radcliffe Trustees in 1770. Five years later it had 94 beds in seven wards and had treated in one year 498 in- and 283 out-patients. Those seeking admission had to appear before the Board of Governors with a recommendation from a subscriber. Many parishes in the county paid a yearly subscription of a few guineas so that they could send their sick poor there. In 1777 it was called a 'modern shewy building' and was criticised for its low ceilings and closed windows. The wards, especially the men's, were 'offensive beyond conception'. It was enlarged and improved several times during the 19th century as more and more people sought medical aid.

Radcliffe Infirmary

There was no provision at the Radcliffe Infirmary for the many cholera victims of the 19th century. In 1832 there were 86 deaths from the disease, in 1849 another 69 and in 1854 a further 115. The outbreaks arose from the appallingly insanitary condition of the city. Reports revealed narrow streets and airless courts of small mean houses with no proper sanitation or pure water supply. In Jericho 'a drain of the filthiest kind runs . . . quite open . . . ten houses and one privy . . . a heap of vegetable matter in one corner'. Health experts recommended drastic measures, 'the dwellings of St. Thomas can only be cleansed by removal; in short, faulty dwellings, faulty ventilation, foul streams, inadequate drainage'.

The Council tried to make good the lack of a pure water supply by the purchase in 1853 of a lake at South Hinksey and the erection of purification works. More and more houses were connected to the supply and the contaminated wells fell into disuse. The Local Board of Health embarked on a main drainage scheme in 1873. Even so, in 1901 as many as 12 families were sharing a single water tap, and three families a water closet.

The unhealthy condition of large parts of the city was due in part to a rapid increase in population, especially between 1821 and 1831, which necessitated the development for housing of some of the low-lying and less suitable areas. In St. Ebbe's parish the market gardens were sold and the area laid out in streets and building plots. Some of the people who moved into the houses were tradesmen who put their hard-earned savings into property. Although the houses were quite well built, the drainage was inadequate and when cholera broke out the disease spread like wildfire.

In St. Thomas's parish the predominantly working-class population

115

*Oxford Tramways
Company horse tram*

increased from over 1,000 in 1801 to well over 8,000 in 1901, and in St. Clement's during the same period from 413 to over 5,000. In the city as a whole the numbers increased from 11,000 in 1801 to 49,000 in 1901. Parishes were divided and new churches built—St. Paul's was opened in 1836 and St. Barnabas's in 1869, to serve the expanding Jericho area.

Expansion in north Oxford was of quite a different type from that elsewhere in the city. In 1770 the Radcliffe Infirmary stood in open countryside and there were only 115 houses in the huge parish of St. Giles. During the second half of the 19th century large houses in spacious gardens were built for college fellows, now permitted to marry, and for wealthier tradesmen wishing to move away from the cramped city centre. This became fashionable Oxford, and represents the heyday of Victorian residential development.

With the growth of the city came the need for public transport, especially for workers, and horse-drawn trams appeared on the streets in 1881. In 1885 it was possible to travel from the railway stations in the Botley Road to the Cowley Road or from Carfax up the Banbury and Kingston Roads for 1*d*.

In the centre of the city, the University and colleges were extending their buildings and clearing large areas which had once housed several hundreds of people. It was these folk who moved out to the new working-class suburbs, leaving the parishes of St. Martin, All Saints, and St. Mary the Virgin, largely depopulated except for academics and students.

There were numerous small tradesmen, tailors, shop keepers, and college servants in Oxford. About 600 men and boys worked at the University Press in 1900, and a few at the small engineering works and Cooper's Oxford Marmalade factory. Incomes were low and the amount of trade depended on the University terms. During the early part of the present century it was quite common for tradesmen to shut their shops during the Long Vacation through lack of customers, 'pockets are empty and the streets deserted'.

There were brighter moments, however. In the 16th century there had been touring players and musicians to amuse people, and for local entertainments and ceremonies there were the City Waits or musicians wearing their liveries and silver badges. During the Commonwealth life was dull and dreary, entertainments were curtailed. The Puritans 'would not suffer any common players to come . . . but what they did by stealth'. After the Restoration the town went mad with excitement; plays were acted at the public houses, or at the Gild Hall or in the Tennis Court. But the theatre came late to Oxford because of the University's opposition. It was feared it would endanger the morals of the students.

116

In the 18th and 19th centuries there were the Oxford Races, held at Portmeadow. It was a time of great excitement, though regarded with strong disapproval by some. 'Booths and vicious living were there about seven weeks . . . as tis abominable that puppet shows and rope dancing should have been this Summer in Oxford to more than two months even just till the races began, corrupting of youths and impoverishing the town'. For the more serious minded there was the public library opened in 1854, and any number of musical, literary, horticultural, and philosophical societies. The highlight of the entertainment year in 19th-century Oxford was St. Giles's Fair, when for two days all might enjoy the music, sideshows and roundabouts, as people still do each September.

XXI   The Changing Face of the University

Sir Thomas Bodley

When Elizabeth I succeeded to the throne in 1558 the University of Oxford bore as little resemblance to its modern counterpart as it had in the late 13th century. Its colleges, administration and finance, its buildings and facilities, the curriculum, and even the students were all to undergo tremendous changes in the centuries following the Reformation which, while not destroying the University's medieval heritage, absorbed and revolutionised it.

After the Reformation, the colleges began to take in and teach an increasing number of undergraduates. Many of the halls of residence closed until there was only one left—St. Edmund Hall. Once there had been 50 or more. Six colleges were founded in the 16th century, proof of the great interest taken in learning by laymen and the need to bolster up the new religion by men trained in its principles. Three more were founded early in the 17th century, before the outbreak of the Civil War. Wadham, built in 1610-13, by Somerset masons, was considered the latest thing in college architecture when completed. Oriel was rebuilt, and other colleges extensively altered, to comply with the new style.

For the University, too, the 16th and early 17th centuries were a time of great building activity, helped by a number of generous benefactors. The library over the Divinity School had been sadly neglected and its books and furniture may have been destroyed by reforming zealots at the time of the Reformation. It was now quite unusable. Sir Thomas Bodley, diplomatist and scholar, who had been a commoner at Magdalen and a Fellow at Merton, paid for its restoration between 1598 and 1602. Then in 1610-13 he financed a much-needed extension—Arts End. It was Bodley who arranged for the library to receive a copy of every book registered at the Stationers' Company of London. Sir John Selden, jurist, antiquary, and M.P. for the University, gave the library his collection of Oriental manuscripts and books and to house them the library was extended by the addition of Selden End in 1636-40. Anthony Wood 'laboured for several weeks' with others to carry the books upstairs and put them on the shelves. Underneath this extension the University built a new meeting room for Congregation.

Thomas Bodley's generosity did not end with his work for the library, which bears his name. He also left money in his will for the

118

completion of the Schools Quad, of which the Divinity School formed one side. The work was finished in 1642, just in time for the buildings to be used by Charles I and his army for storing arms and food.

The Schools were meant to be the teaching headquarters of the University, but they were already something of an anachronism when completed, for instruction was coming more and more into the hands of colleges. By the end of the 18th century the Bodleian, always short of space, began to expand into the Schools, until in the 19th century the whole complex was being used for library purposes.

William Laud, Chancellor of Oxford University

Henry Danvers, Earl of Danby, was another benefactor whose gift to the University has brought it fame. He bought the site of the Jews' Burying Ground, opposite Magdalen College, and had it converted into the Physic, or Botanic, Garden for the study and growing of herbs, especially medicinal ones, the first such garden in England. The level of the ground had to be raised to prevent flooding before it could be opened in 1621. Celia Fiennes visited the garden later in the 17th century and found it 'afforded great diversion and pleasure, the variety of flowers and plants would have entertained one a week . . .'.

In spite of this immense building programme and the interest being taken by laymen in learning, all was far from satisfactory in the University. The upheavals of the Reformation had left their mark. The dangers of opposing the royal will in religious affairs had been brought home to all by the burning at the stake of Cranmer, Ridley, and Latimer. No monarch could afford to have a dissenting University, for its influence was great both in religious and secular spheres. In 1576 all students wishing to take their degrees had to subscribe to the 39 Articles and in 1580 all had to take the Oath of Supremacy. Those whose convictions prevented them from doing so had no alternative but to go. Many erudite men, like the Jesuit, Edmund Campion, had to depart, leaving the University the poorer for it.

During the Commonwealth, a similar situation arose when Royalist sympathisers were ejected. After 1660 this was reversed—the Parliamentarians were ousted and the Royalists reinstated. The damage done to scholarship was considerable. 'As for learning of these persons thus restored you cannot expect that it should be much, because the most part of them were forc'd in the interval to gain a bare livelihood, and there so far from increasing that knowledge they had, that they lost it'. So Anthony Wood summed it up.

Although the Restoration of the Monarchy led to a fall in the standard of scholarship, building started up again. Christopher Wren, who was a student at Wadham, Fellow of All Souls, and Savilian Professor of Astronomy, designed Tom Tower for Christ Church in 1682, and part of the Garden Quad at Trinity. His most important

119

Doorway to the Old Ashmolean

work in Oxford was the Sheldonian Theatre, completed in 1669. He used as his model the semi-circular Roman theatre. Inside, the ceiling was designed to suggest the open sky. Gilbert Sheldon, Chancellor of the University, and later Archbishop of Canterbury, gave £1,000 towards the scheme for a more suitable setting for major University ceremonies than the church of St. Mary the Virgin. But it failed to attract other gifts, and Sheldon bore the whole cost of over £12,200 himself.

Next door to the Sheldonian, facing on to Broad Street, was built in 1678-83, the first public museum in England—the Old Ashmolean. It was named after Elias Ashmole, antiquarian, and founder member of the Royal Society. He gave his collection of natural history curiosities together with those of the John Tradescants, father and son, which he had inherited, to the University on condition they were put on display. Twelve cartloads of rarities were delivered to the museum and put on show in one of the largest rooms. The museum also accommodated the School of Natural History and a laboratory 'furnished with all sorts of furnaces and other necessary materials'. This was the first laboratory in the University and is evidence of a growing interest in scientific studies. The first custodian of the museum was Robert Plot, Professor of Chemistry, and author of *The Natural History of Oxfordshire*.

The last two buildings to go up in this part of Oxford, which from the early days of the University had been its administrative, ceremonial, and teaching centre, were not erected until the first half of the 18th century. The Clarendon Building was completed in 1714 and housed the University Press, which had outgrown its accommodation in the Sheldonian Theatre. The money for it came largely from the gift to the University of the profits of *The History of the Great Rebellion,* a best-seller, written by Edward Hyde, the first Earl of Clarendon, and former Chancellor of the University. His son gave the University its copyright. The Press moved out in 1830 to new premises in Walton Street, leaving the Clarendon Building to be used as offices.

The Physic library, better known now as the Radcliffe Camera, was given to the University by Dr. John Radcliffe. He chose as the site the area between the Schools Quad, and St. Mary the Virgin church, which at that time was occupied by numerous gardens and small cottages. These had to be bought up and cleared by the Radcliffe Trustees, and the library, a massive, circular, domed building, was not opened until 1749.

The Radcliffe Trustees had money to spare and some of it was spent on building, between 1772 and 1775, the Observatory in the Woodstock Road, a very fine and interesting building, modelled on

39.   The English Agricultural Society's showyard at Oxford, 1839. The show was held on pasture land, now Mansfield College, belonging to a local wealthy butcher, Mr. Pinfold. About 15,000 noblemen and gentlemen attended. Later the society became the Royal Agricultural Society of England.

OXFORD IN THE FUTURE, OR THE NEW FRESHMAN.

NAVVY. "GALLON O' AUDIT ALE, GUV'NOR, PLEASE. I'S GOT T'BLUNT TO PAY VOR'N."

40.   Feelings ran high locally and nationally for and against the G.W.R. Company's plan to build a carriage works in Oxford. Punch ridiculed the idea.

41. St. Clement's, Oxford. The church was demolished in 1827-9 and rebuilt on another site. Behind it are the toll house and gate, Magdalen Bridge and Magdalen College tower.

42. Carfax, Oxford. A church dedicated to St. Martin stood here before the Norman Conquest. The church pictured here was built in 1820-2 and then demolished, except for the tower, in 1896 to widen the busy cross roads.

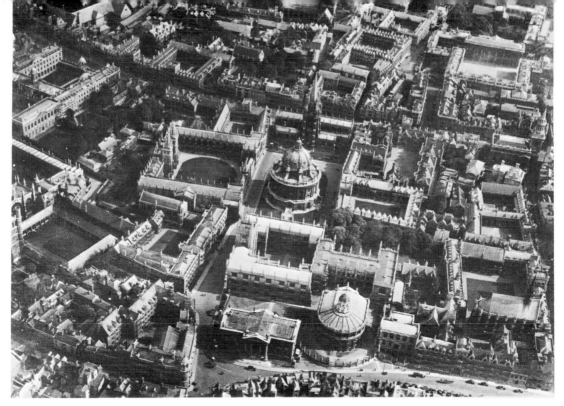

43.   Academic Oxford, the heart of the university town. In the centre of the photograph
is the Radcliffe Camera.

44.   In strong contrast, industrial Oxford. In the 1930s the success of the car works at Cowley,
seen here, led to the rapid expansion of the suburbs.

45. St. Giles' Fair in 1907 looking south towards St. Michael at the Northgate. The fair seems to date from the seventeenth century.

46. The construction of the M40 motorway has opened up this view of the south Oxfordshire plain from the cutting through the Chilterns.

the Temple of the Winds at Athens. It is no longer used for its original purpose.

On the whole, the 18th century saw Oxford, except in the matter of building, at a low ebb and the University's reputation sank. William of Orange and the early Hanoverian kings were unpopular in University circles. Party feelings ran high and its members got caught up in politics. In 1705 the Duchess of Marlborough rebuked 'the Members of that University's being so hot in relation to the present administration of affairs . . .'. The standard of learning and teaching fell. Professorships had become little more than sinecures; the curriculum was old fashioned; the disputations which preceded the granting of degrees had degenerated so far as to be quite meaningless. Colleges had become very powerful and very wealthy. They challenged the authority of the comparatively poor University and contributed nothing towards its running costs. Heads of Colleges formed the Hebdomadal Board, the chief executive committee of the University's administration. Complaints were constantly being made about the students' behaviour and drunkenness, of too much time spent in coffee houses or pleasure-seeking. William Freke, who came up in 1619 for three years, bought 22 pairs of boots and shoes and had music lessons, but spent hardly anything on books. A century later Erasmus Phillips, up for only a year, wasted his time at the Oxford, Burford, Woodstock, and Bicester races. Edward Gibbon considered his sojourn at Magdalen 'the most idle and unprofitable' time of his life. Men of scholarship—Joseph Addison of Magdalen, Samuel Johnson of Pembroke, and Adam Smith of Balliol—were the exception rather than the rule.

Radcliffe Observatory

Part of the trouble stemmed from the Laudian Code set down in 1636 by William Laud, Chancellor of the University. He completely revised the University statutes, and regulations were made covering every aspect of academic life, including rules against the wearing of curls and immoderately long hair, the playing of 'dibs, dice, and cards', and football. Unfortunately, the Code perpetuated a curriculum that was already old-fashioned when laid down, and there seemed to be no way of developing or expanding it to meet new ideas and demands.

Reform came gradually. The first big step was taken in 1800 when new examination statutes, establishing pass and honours degrees, were introduced. This encouraged competition, especially among the better students. New Schools were set up, scholarships and fellowships were opened to all comers. Acts of Parliament of 1854 and 1877 reconstituted the government of the University and reorganised its finances. Colleges were made to contribute money towards the University's work.

121

The University Museum

The last half of the 19th century saw a tremendous revival in learning, and facilities for study were greatly expanded. Keble, founded in 1870, was the first entirely new foundation for 250 years. It was established as a memorial to John Keble, as a college where men of limited means could be taught under the influence of the Church of England. The college was built of red brick with coloured patterning and was as startling to Victorian eyes as it has been to succeeding generations. Campion Hall was established in 1896 for the Society of Jesus—religious tests having been removed in 1871. In 1879 two residential halls were opened for women, though they were not admitted to degrees until 1922. In 1899 Ruskin Hall was founded by two Americans for working men and women, and in the same year Cecil Rhodes made provision in his will for 60 scholarships for men from the British Empire, U.S.A., and Germany. These men, chosen for athletic prowess as well as for academic ability, greatly encouraged sport in the University. The foundation of new colleges has continued and their buildings have aroused interest and considerable comment, not always favourable.

The opening of the University Museum in 1860 marked a new period in University buildings and activities. Until then opportunities for studying science were very limited, and Sir Henry Acland worked hard for years to improve them; it was largely due to his activities that the museum was built. There were public display rooms and other private accommodation for the study of zoology, mineralogy, geology, and other subjects. Elias Ashmole's collections were removed from the Old Ashmolean to the new museum, and the remainder went to the University Galleries in Beaumont Street, the forerunner of the present Ashmolean Museum, and to the Pitt-Rivers Museum. Since 1935 the Old Ashmolean has housed the Museum of the History of Science and the collection contains many rare scientific instruments.

The Bodleian Library, like everything else in the University, was expanding rapidly, having received gifts of many valuable books and manuscripts. It took over the Radcliffe Camera, and in 1937 the New Bodleian Library was opened. The Bodleian now possesses over 3,000,000 books and over 50,000 manuscripts.

Today the University is open to all men and women of ability who are able to meet the entrance requirements. Numbers have increased and living accommodation is always hard to find. In 1570 the University had about 1,700 members; in 1970 there were over 9,000 undergraduates alone. Great expansion has taken place in teaching to meet the demands of government, trade and industry, health, and defence. The emphasis in recent years has tended to be towards the study of science, and the area around the University

122

Museum has been built up with laboratories. The University plays a very important part in medical research as a result of the generosity of William Morris, Lord Nuffield. In the 1930s he gave millions of pounds for the foundation of the Nuffield Medical School and the Nuffield Institute of Medical Research. Lord Nuffield recognised that there existed a wide gap between academics and laymen interested in, and concerned with, the same problems. To help bridge this gap, he endowed Nuffield College in 1937, where both groups might work together. This idea has given direction to much of the research work conducted in the University and the retiring Vice-Chancellor in 1973 recommended that the University as a whole should strengthen its contacts with the outside world, especially in business and industrial spheres. University scholarship has come a long way from the medieval concept of the search for knowledge for its own sake.

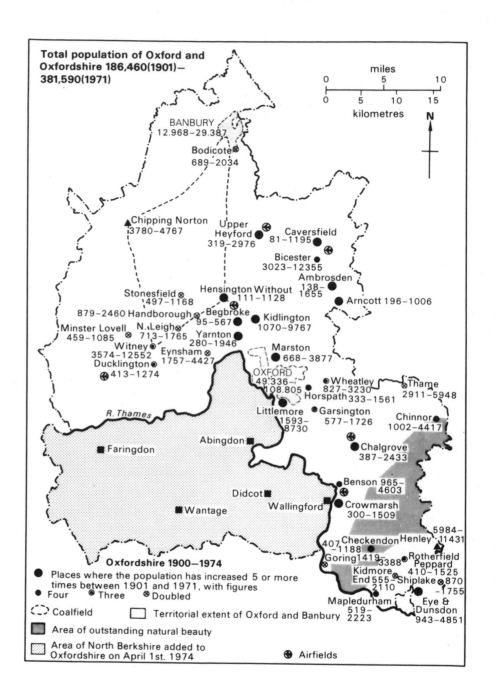

Total population of Oxford and Oxfordshire 186,460(1901)–381,590(1971)

miles
0   5   10

0   5   10   15
kilometres

N

BANBURY
12.968–29.387

Bodicote
689–2034

Chipping Norton
3780–4767

Upper Heyford
319–2976

Caversfield
81–1195

Bicester
3023–12355

Ambrosden
138–1655

Arncott 196–1006

Stonesfield
497–1168

Hensington Without
111–1128

879–2460 Handborough

Begbroke
95–567

Kidlington
1070–9767

Minster Lovell
459–1085

N. Leigh
713–1765

Yarnton
280–1946

Witney
3574–12552

Eynsham
1757–4427

Ducklington
413–1274

Marston
668–3877

OXFORD
49.336–108.805

Wheatley
827–3230

Thame
2911–5948

Horspath
333–1561

Littlemore
1593–8730

Garsington
577–1726

Chinnor
1002–4417

Chalgrove
387–2433

Faringdon

R. Thames

Abingdon

Benson 965–4603

Didcot

Wallingford

Crowmarsh
300–1509

Wantage

Checkendon
407–1188

Henley
5984–11431

Goring1419–3388

Rotherfield Peppard
410–1525

Kidmore End 555–2110

Shiplake
870–1755

Mapledurham
519–2223

Eye & Dunsdon
943–4851

Oxfordshire 1900–1974

● Places where the population has increased 5 or more times between 1901 and 1971, with figures
● Four   ⊛ Three   ⊗ Doubled

⬭ Coalfield   ☐ Territorial extent of Oxford and Banbury

▓ Area of outstanding natural beauty

░ Area of North Berkshire added to Oxfordshire on April 1st. 1974

⊛ Airfields

124

XXII Oxfordshire, 1900–1974

By 1900 Oxfordshire was stagnating. Agriculture was still suffering from the effects of the depression it had gone through in the late 19th century. From being one of the richest counties in England, it had become one of the poorer, and in 1911 its farm labourers received the lowest wages of all such workers in England.

Chinnor lime kilns

Part of the county's poverty was due to the lack of any industrial revolution within its boundaries in the late 18th and early 19th centuries. Domestic crafts which provided many labouring families with a little extra money, were unable to compete with the mass-produced, machine-made goods. Work became scarce. The cement and lime works founded at Chinnor in 1908, and another at Shipton-on-Cherwell, were only very small concerns employing no more than a handful of men. The extraction of iron ore in and around Hook Norton, Wroxton, and Bloxham did not get under way on any scale until 1917. Old trades came to an end. Less and less stone was quarried and the Stonesfield slates were not made after 1904. The blanket industry at Witney and the tweed mill at Chipping Norton provided around 1,000 jobs. The plush factory at Shutford had an excellent export trade and claimed in 1910 to be the largest firm of its kind in the world, but the 1914-18 war seriously affected foreign sales. It was sold up in 1948. In 1921 agriculture was the largest employer and of every 1,000 people in Oxfordshire at that time, 234 worked on the land.

Poor work prospects and low wages encouraged emigration, not only to the U.S.A. and Commonwealth countries, but also to the manufacturing and industrial towns in England. The rate of increase of the population of Oxfordshire began to fall. In 1801 there were 111,977 people living in the county and in 1841 the number had risen to 163,127. In 1901 this figure had only increased by another 18,000, a rate of growth of no more than 11 per cent., whereas the population of England and Wales as a whole more than doubled during those 60 years.

In 1973, the last full year before local government reorganisation changed the shape and size of the county, Oxfordshire presented a very different image from that of 1900. The population had greatly increased; the towns were prosperous and expanding; Oxford was one of the wealthier cities in England; there were some large and profitable farms, and the livestock market at Banbury was the largest in Europe.

125

An early Morris motor

Oxfordshire was transformed by an 'industrial revolution' that was unexpected, unplanned, and at first unnoticed. Its results have been far-reaching and widely felt. In 1912 William Morris, created Lord Nuffield in 1938, who had had in turn a cycle and motor-cycle repair shop in the High Street and a garage specialising in car repairs at the corner of Longwall and Holywell in Oxford, opened a workshop in Cowley and called his new firm Morris Motors. In the same year the first Morris car was produced. Morris's company flourished, and in 1926 Pressed Steel moved into Cowley to make car bodies.

Not only did the car industry provide urgently needed employment for local people, but its rapid growth attracted a large number of outsiders to Oxford. Between 1921 and 1931 the city's population increased by no fewer than 13,249, a rate of growth only exceeded by two other places in England. In 1936, 43 per cent. of the male insured workers in Oxford were new to the county. They required homes and building trades expanded and flourished. The area east of the Cherwell was quickly built up, and the small villages of Old Headington, Headington Quarry, Iffley, and others were soon joined to Oxford by a continuous belt of housing and the city boundary was extended to include them. In 1946 planners suggested that Oxford had become too big and that it should be divided into two towns, separated by the river Cherwell. By 1951 Oxford's population was 98,684.

People in and around the city became better-off than they had ever been, but the continuing prosperity of Oxford has become dependent to an alarming extent on the success of one industry and a number of associated firms. During the slump of the 1930s there was virtually no unemployment in Oxford, for there was an ever-expanding market for cars, but when war broke out in 1939 there were many men out of work in Oxford owing to the fall in demand for cars. More recently during slumps in the industry, the extraordinary situation has arisen of 50 men competing for the job of grave-digger. The higher wages to be had in Oxford lured many agricultural labourers away from the land and farmers have found it increasingly difficult to keep their workers.

Work opportunities also greatly improved at Banbury during the 1930s even though the Tweed Company closed in 1932, and Samuelson's Britannia Works in 1933. The town was transformed by the opening of the Northern Aluminium Company's factory and good rail and road communications. The company's rapid growth attracted new people to the town, and its population, which had increased by only 613 people between 1921 and 1931, grew by nearly 5,000 in the next 20 years. In the 1950s the Banbury Borough Council established an industrial estate and attracted many firms to the town, including General Foods Ltd. in 1965.

126

Bicester also has good rail and road communications and in recent years has grown well beyond its market town status. It is an important Ordnance Depot for the Ministry of Defence and has both an army barracks and an R.A.F. station.

New people continue to move into Oxfordshire as part of a deliberate policy. Banbury is an overspill town for Birmingham and London, and a population of 40,000 is planned by 1981. Bicester, too, has taken in people from London and by 1981 it is expected to be a town of 21,000, nearly double what it was in 1971. In 1971 the total population of the county was 309,452 compared with 189,615 in 1901, a rate of growth considerably above that for England and Wales as a whole.

This influx of people has meant more and more houses, and the tendency has been for the traditional building materials to be replaced by the mass-produced, changing the character of many towns and villages. In spite of its growth, Oxfordshire remains essentially a rural county. Its hunts, especially the Bicester and Heythrop, are well known. Large amounts of land, however, are gradually being given over to industrial and other non-rural pursuits, and there are already many disfiguring features on the landscape, let alone those that are planned for the future. Traffic is a major problem both in the towns and countryside. When completed the M40 motorway will run through the county carrying traffic from the Midlands to London, always an important route. New roads like this one take valuable agricultural land and change the face of the countryside. By the end of the century Otmoor may have been turned into a vast water reservoir, and there are plans to drill for oil and gas at Berrick Prior. Recently, a vast coalfield, which stretches from Banbury to Witney and from Chipping Norton to Woodstock, has been identified. Its exploitation would mean enough coal to meet the whole of Britain's current needs for this fuel for at least 70 years. What it would mean to Oxfordshire remains to be seen, but the prospect of large-scale coal production in what is one of the most attractive parts of the county, is an alarming one. The civil airport at Kidlington is used to train pilots and Upper Heyford is the home of a U.S.A.A.F. unit and Brize Norton of the R.A.F.

When William Cobbett rode through Oxfordshire in the 1820s he declared it to be 'A very poor, dull and uninteresting country all the way', and he did not approve of Oxford or its University. Other people have thought, and still do think, differently, and Oxford is after London probably one of the biggest tourist attractions in England. Agas in the 17th century declared Oxford to be 'A citie seated rich in everything. Girt with wood and water, pasture, corn and mill'. Quiller-Couch thought it 'more beautiful than all his

Banbury Cross

Oxford Preservation Trust's houses

dreams', and Baedeker's Guide for 1887 recommended that unless visitors could go to both Oxford and Cambridge, they should go only to Oxford—'on the whole more attractive'. The extra traffic created by tourists in Oxford has brought its problems, and much of the centre of the city has now been reserved for pedestrians. In 1927 the Oxford Preservation Trust was founded for 'the preservation of open spaces and good architecture in and around Oxford and the creation of new amenities', while, more recently, societies have been formed for the preservation of Victorian north Oxford from the hands of developers. In 1967 the Oxford Archaeological Excavation Committee was established to record as much as possible of Oxford's past during the rebuilding of St. Ebbe's and other sites in the city. This work has now been extended to cover the whole county.

Visitors to Oxford usually combine it with a trip to nearby Blenheim Palace which has been something of a curiosity ever since it was first built. In 1711 when the Duke of Marlborough visited the site to see how the building work was proceeding, it was necessary 'to keep people back from crowding in'. It was opened to the public during George III's reign at a time of day that would not disturb the afternoon rest of the duke's children. The annual international regatta held at Henley attracts an increasing number of spectators each year, and now the Thames and Chilterns Tourist Board encourages people to extend the time spent sight-seeing in the county to include other places and events.

The Oxfordshire with which this book has been concerned came to an end as a constitutional unit on 1st April 1974. From that date the new Oxfordshire, with its boundaries extended to include a large part of north Berkshire, came into existence, and the curious elongated shape that the county has presented for over 1,000 years finally disappeared from the map. Whether the new county will outlast the next 1,000 years seems, somehow, unlikely.

128

Select Bibliography

The bibliography included here is intended only as a brief guide to the extensive literature available on all aspects of the history of Oxfordshire.

Those who wish to read more about the history of a particular place in, or subject connected with, Oxfordshire, are recommended to consult *A Bibliography of Printed Works relating to Oxfordshire* (1955) and *A Bibliography of Printed Works relating to the University of Oxford* (1968), both compiled by E. H. Cordeaux and D. H. Merry. A similar bibliography for the city of Oxford is being assembled.

Nine volumes of the *Victoria History of the County of Oxford* have been completed. Volume I (1939) contains sections on the prehistory and political history of the county; an account of the grammar and pre-1800 elementary schools; and a translation of that part of Domesday Book relating to Oxfordshire. Volume II (1907) has articles on the ecclesiastical (including the religious houses), the social and economic, and the industrial and agricultural development in Oxfordshire. Volume III (1954) relates the history of the University. Volumes V-X (1957-1972) describe the history of all the parishes in the hundreds of Bullingdon, Ploughley, Dorchester and Thame, Lewknor and Pyrton, Bloxham, and Banbury. When finished, the series will form the major reference work for the history of the City, University and County of Oxford.

A number of societies exist for the publication of records, documents, and articles concerned with the history of the county. The most important are (with date of earliest publication):

Oxford Historical Society (1884) historical records of the University and City of Oxford.
Oxfordshire Record Society (1919) documents relating to the history of Oxfordshire.
Oxoniensia (1936) archaeology, history, and architecture of Oxford and its neighbourhood.
Banbury Historical Society (1960) records of Banbury and neighbourhood.

The books produced and published by these societies contain such a wealth of material on such a wide variety of subjects that it is impossible to list their contents here.

Iron Age bone comb, Stanton Harcourt

OXFORDSHIRE

(Arranged in the order of the chapters of this book)

Martin, A. F. and Steel, R. W., *The Oxford Region, a scientific and historical survey* (1954).
Plot, R., *The Natural History of Oxfordshire* (1677).
Skelton, J., *The Antiquities of Oxfordshire* (1823).

Harding, D. W., *The Iron Age in the Upper Thames Basin* (1972).

Gelling, M., *The Place-names of Oxfordshire, E.P.N.S.* xxiii-xxiv (1953-4).

Allison, K. J., Beresford, M. W., and Hurst, J. G., *The deserted villages of Oxfordshire*, University College of Leicester, Dept. of Eng. Local History, Occasional Paper. 17 (1965).

Ballard, A., *The Black death on the manors of Witney*, Oxf. Studies in Social and Legal History, V (1916).

Colvin, H. M., ed., *The History of the King's Works* (1963).

Gray, H. L., *The later history of the Midland system in Oxfordshire* (1915).

Harvey, P., *A medieval Oxfordshire village: Cuxham, 1240-1400* (1965).

Jope, E. M. and Terrett, I. B., 'Oxfordshire' in *Domesday geography of south-east England*, ed. H. C. Darby and E. M. J. Campbell (1962).

Orwin, C. S. and C. S., *The open fields* (1938).

Renn, D. F., *Norman castles in Britain* (1968).

Bird, W. H., *Old Oxfordshire churches* (1932).

Brookes, J., *Mid-Oxfordshire churches* (1970).

Ballard, A., *Chronicles of the Royal borough of Woodstock* (1896).

Beesley, A., *The History of Banbury* (1841).

Beresford, M. W., *New towns of the Middle Ages; town plantation in England, Wales and Gascony* (1967).

Burn, J. S., *A history of Henley-on-Thames* (1861).

Cockburn, A. E., *Corporations of England and Wales*, i (1835).

Colvin, H. M., *A history of Deddington* (1963).

Gretton, M. S., *Burford, past and present* (1950).

Gretton, R. H., *The Burford records, a study in a minor town government* (1920).

Giles, J. A., *History of the parish and town of Bampton* (1848).

Giles, J. A., *History of Witney* (1852).

Meades, E., *The history of Chipping Norton* (1949).

Monk, W. J., *History of Witney* (1894).

Oldfield, T. H. B., *An entire and complete history, political and personal, of the boroughs of Great Britain* (1792).

Potts, W., *History of Banbury* (1958).

Brown, J. Howard, *A short history of Thame School* (1927).

Carlisle, N., *Concise description of endowed Grammar Schools*, ii (1818).

Thomas, V., *Account of the night-march of Charles the First from Oxford* (1850).

Toynbee, M. and Young, P., *Cropredy Bridge, 1644, the campaign and battle* (1970).

Varley, F. J., *The seige of Oxford, 1642-46* (1932).

Besse, J., *A collection of the sufferings of the people called Quakers* (1753).

Braithwaite, W. C., *First planting of Quakerism in Oxfordshire* (1908).

Green, V. H., *The young Mr. Wesley: a study of John Wesley and Oxford* (1961).

McClatchey, D., *Oxfordshire clergy, 1777-1869* (1960).

Emery, F., *The Oxfordshire Lancscape* (1974).

Gray, H. L., 'Yeoman farming in Oxfordshire from the sixteenth century to the nineteenth', *Quart. Journ. of Econ.* (1910).

Havinden, M. A., 'Agricultural progress in open-field Oxfordshire', *Essays in Agrarian History*, i, ed. W. E. Minchinton (1968). .

Higgs, J., 'Farming in the Oxfordshire region from the Napoleonic Wars to the World Wars', *Journ. Roy. Agric. Soc.* (1958).

Leadam, I. S., *The Domesday of Inclosures, 1517-18* (1897).

Marshall, M., 'Oxfordshire', *The report of the land utilisation survey of Britain*, part 56 (1943).

Read, C. S., 'On the farming of Oxfordshire', *Journ. Roy. Agric. Soc.* (1854).

Young, A., *A view of the agriculture of Oxfordshire* (1809).

Arkell, W. J., *Oxford stone* (1947).

Beckinsale, R. P., 'Factors in the development of the Cotswold woollen industry', *The Geographical Journ.* (1937).

Plummer, A., *The Witney blanket industry, the records of the Witney blanket weavers* (1934).

Plummer, A. and Early, R. E., *The blanket makers, 1669-1969; a history of Charles Early and Marriot (Witney) Ltd.* (1969).

Sibbitt, C., *Bells, blankets, baskets, and boats; a survey of crafts and industries in Oxfordshire*, Oxford City and County Museum, Pub. 1 (1968).

Williams, W. R. J., *The Parliamentary history of the county of Oxford . . . 1213-1899* (1899).

Hadfield, C., *The canals of the East Midlands* (1970).

MacDermott, E. T. (revised by C. R. Clinker), *History of the Great Western Railway* (1964).

Thacker, F. S., *The Thames highway, a history of the inland navigation* (1914).

Howard, J., *State of Prisons* (1784).

Eden, F. M., *The state of the Poor* (1797).

Oldham, C. R., 'Oxfordshire poor laws', *Econ. Hist. Rev.* (1932-4; 1934-5).

Historic Oxfordshire, Oxfordshire Rural Community Council (1951).

Orr, J., *Agriculture in Oxfordshire* (1916).

Sherwood, Jennifer and Pevsner, Nikolaus, *The Buildings of England: Oxfordshire* (1974).

Woods, K. S., *The rural industries round Oxford, a survey* (1921).

THE CITY AND UNIVERSITY OF OXFORD

Butler, C. V., *Social conditions in Oxford* (1912).

Emden, A. B., *An Oxford hall in Medieval Times* (1927).

Fasnacht, R., *A history of the city of Oxford* (1954).

Gibson, A. G., *The Radcliffe Infirmary* (1926).

Gilbert, E. W., 'The industrialization of Oxford', *The Geographical Journ.* (1947).

Handbook to the University of Oxford (1969).

Hassall, T. G., *Oxford, the city beneath your feet* (1972).

Ingram, J., *Memorials of Oxford* (1837).

Jope, E. M., 'Saxon Oxford and its region', *Dark-age Britain*, ed. D. B. Harden (1956).

Rashdall, H., *Universities of Europe in the Middle Ages*, ii, ed. F. M. Powicke and A. B. Emden (1936).

Royal Commission on Historical Monuments: *An Inventory of the Historical Monuments in the City of Oxford* (1939).

Turner, W. H., *Records of the city of Oxford, 1509-83* (1880).

Index